D0031896

Hot & Spicy Recipes

Hot
&
Spicy
Recipes

P
· PARRAGON ·

First published in Great Britain in 1999 by
Parragon
Queen Street House
4-5 Queen Street
Bath
BA1 1HE

ISBN: 0-7525-2922-6

Produced by Haldane Mason, London

Printed in Italy

Material in this book has previously appeared in
What's Cooking? Chinese, What's Cooking? Indian,
What's Cooking? Wok, and *What's Cooking? Thai*

Note
Cup measurements in this book are for
American cups. Tablespoons are assumed to be
15 ml. Unless otherwise stated, milk is assumed
to be full fat, eggs are medium and
pepper is freshly ground black pepper.

Contents

Introduction 6

Soups & Starters 10

Poultry & Meat 48

Fish & Seafood 108

Vegetable Dishes 146

Rice, Noodles,
Pulses & Breads 180

Desserts 222

Index 238

Introduction

Indian, Chinese and Thai cuisines are enjoyed all over the world and it is now easier than ever to recreate authentic dishes at home. Supermarkets stock an impressive range of the special ingredients that are required for these types of cuisine.

However, it is only in the last twenty years or so that the majority of people in the West have become generally aware of spicy, Eastern cuisine. This is mostly due to the proliferation of Indian, Chinese, and more recently Thai restaurants in towns and cities throughout the world.

It is advisable to buy a selection of five or six spices and vary the quantities to bring out flavours you particularly like or to adjust the hotness. You can also buy ready-made spice mixtures and other seasonings, such as Thai green curry paste, and an enormous range of sauces to add to stir-fries – for example Black Bean Sauce or Sweet & Sour Sauce. Indian and Thai dishes are quick to prepare since they are mostly cooked in a wok. On the other hand, Indian food usually requires longer cooking times but since the flavour of curries is improved when reheated large quantities can be cooked and stored, and then reheated when required.

Unlike in the West where it is traditional to serve the same dish to everyone, it is usual in the East to serve a variety of dishes which the guests can share. It is also important that the dishes complement each other, so whenever there is a hot dish, a milder dish should also be served.

Nearly every kitchen boasts a wok, and this is the perfect recipe book to help you make better use of this most versatile and healthy cooking tool. The clever design of a wok makes it very versatile; as well as stir-frying, it is also excellent for steaming, braising and deep-frying. It is essential to heat the wok before adding the food to ensure quick and even cooking. As the food cooks so quickly, you will need to prepare everything before you start to cook or the first ingredients will be overcooked before the others are ready to add.

There are four regional schools of Chinese cooking and each has a set of distinctive flavours and aromas. Cantonese is the best known of these cuisines, and uses light and subtle flavourings in contrast to the fiery Szechuan dishes and the rich Shanghai recipes. Bejing cuisine depends more on dried and smoked ingredients due to the harsh winters in that area.

Thailand has a rich and abundant cuisine that has changed little over the centuries despite regular foreign intervention. Today it still stands independent to gastronomic scrutiny and fares the better for it. It is not difficult to spot the influence of near neighbours like China and India in stir-fries and curries but somehow they are given the unmistakable Thai treatment with herbs, spices and coconut milk. So it is easy to see how on the one hand Thai cuisine can be described as light, aromatic and zestful, yet on the other hot, robust and full-blooded!

For many there is an art to Indian cooking; dealing with over thirty different spices and flavourings can be intimidating, but the tastes and smells drifting up from your pans will encourage you to continue. The spices themselves are called masalas. Once ground together, masalas can keep for approximately two months, but it is best to mix and use them as freshly as possible.

Garam Masala is often used in the recipes in this book and involves grinding the following spices together: 1 tsp cardamom seeds, 2 tsp cloves, 2 tbsp cumin seeds, 2 tbsp coriander seeds, 2 dried bay leaves, 7.5 cm/3 inch cinnamon stick, 1 tbsp black peppercorns and 1 dried red chilli. It is advisable to prepare your dishes in advance as the spices and flavourings will take time to develop their full potential. Make the dish in advance and leave it overnight or for up to three days in the refrigerator before being re-heated.

A common accompaniment to spicy dishes is Cucumber Raita. This is simple to make – mix together 250 g/8 oz/1 cup natural yogurt, 2 tsp chopped fresh mint, 175 g/6 oz cucumber, peeled, deseeded and cut into matchsticks, and salt to taste.

When planning a menu for a shared meal, allow one dish per person. Always increase the number of dishes rather than the quantity of ingredients when cooking for a large number of people, as this will give more variety and contrast in taste, colour and flavour on the table.

This book contains a wide selection of dishes, ranging from soups and starters to main meals, side dishes and even desserts to cool the taste buds. Each dish is photographed in full colour, so you can see just how delicious these recipes are.

Soups & Starters

Soup is not served as a separate course in China and Thailand, but for those who prefer to eat in a Western way, these soups make a delicious appetiser. The other dishes in this chapter are perfect for tempting the taste buds at the beginning of a meal, but they are so versatile they can be used to add interest to a buffet.

Chicken Soup with Almonds

This soup can also be made using turkey or pheasant breasts. Pheasant gives a stronger, gamey flavour.

SERVES 4

1 large or 2 small boned and skinned chicken breasts
1 tbsp sunflower oil
1 carrot, cut into julienne strips
4 spring onions (scallions), thinly sliced diagonally
750 ml/ 1¼ pints/ 3 cups chicken stock
finely grated rind of ½ lemon
45 g/ 1½ oz/ ⅓ cup ground almonds
1 tbsp light soy sauce
1 tbsp lemon juice
30 g/ 1 oz/ ¼ cup flaked (slivered) almonds, toasted
salt and pepper

1 Cut each breast into 4 strips lengthways, then slice very thinly across the grain to give chicken shreds.

2 Heat the oil in the wok, swirling it around until really hot. Add the chicken and toss for 3–4 minutes until sealed and almost cooked through. Then add the carrot and continue to cook for 2–3 minutes, stirring all the time. Add the spring onions (scallions) and stir.

3 Add the stock to the wok and bring to the boil.

Add the lemon rind, ground almonds, soy sauce, lemon juice and plenty of seasoning. Bring back to the boil and simmer, uncovered, for 5 minutes, stirring occasionally.

4 Add most of the toasted flaked (slivered) almonds and continue to cook for a further 1–2 minutes. Season to taste.

5 Serve the soup very hot, in individual bowls, sprinkled with the remaining toasted almonds.

Fish & Vegetable Soup

**This chunky fish soup flavoured with
ginger and lemon makes a meal in itself.**

SERVES 4

250 g/8 oz white fish fillets, such as cod, halibut, haddock, sole
½ tsp ground ginger • ½ tsp salt
1 small leek, trimmed and sliced
2–4 crab sticks (optional), defrosted if frozen
1 tbsp sunflower oil • 1 large carrot, cut into julienne strips
8 canned water chestnuts, sliced thinly
1.25 litres/2¼ pints/5 cups fish or vegetable stock
1 tbsp lemon juice • 1 tbsp light soy sauce
1 large courgette (zucchini), cut into julienne strips • pepper

1 Remove any skin from the fish and cut the fish into cubes, about 2.5 cm/1 inch. Combine the ground ginger and salt and rub into the fish. Leave to marinate for at least 30 minutes.

2 Meanwhile, divide the green and white parts of the leek. Cut each part into 2.5 cm/1 inch lengths and then into julienne strips, keeping the two parts separate. Slice the crab sticks into 1 cm/½ inch pieces.

3 Heat the oil in the wok, swirling it around so it is really hot. Add the white part of the leek and stir-fry for 2 minutes, then add the carrots and water chestnuts and cook for 1–2 minutes more, stirring thoroughly. Add the stock and bring to the boil, then add the lemon juice and soy sauce and simmer for 2 minutes.

4 Add the fish and continue to cook for about 5 minutes until the fish begins to break up a little, then add the green part of the leek and the courgettes (zucchini) and simmer for about 1 minute. Add the sliced crab sticks, if using, and season to taste with pepper. Simmer for 1–2 minutes and serve piping hot.

Prawn (Shrimp) Soup

A mixture of textures and flavours make this an interesting and colourful soup. The egg may be made into a flat omelette and added as thin strips.

SERVES 4

2 tbsp sunflower oil
2 spring onions (scallions), sliced thinly diagonally
1 carrot, grated coarsely
125 g/ 4 oz large closed cup mushrooms, sliced thinly
1 litre/ 1¾ pints/ 4 cups fish or vegetable stock
½ tsp Chinese five-spice powder
1 tbsp light soy sauce
125 g/ 4 oz large peeled prawns (shrimp) or peeled tiger prawns (shrimp), defrosted if frozen
½ bunch of watercress, trimmed and chopped roughly
1 egg, beaten well • salt and pepper
4 large prawns (shrimp) in shells, to garnish (optional)

1 Heat the oil in a wok, swirling it around until really hot. Add the spring onions (scallions) and stir-fry for 1 minute then add the carrots and mushrooms and continue to cook for about 2 minutes.

2 Add the stock and bring to the boil then season to taste with salt and pepper, five-spice powder and soy sauce. Simmer for 5 minutes.

3 If the prawns (shrimp) are really large, cut them in half before adding to the wok, then continue to simmer for 3–4 minutes.

4 Add the watercress to the wok and mix well, then slowly pour in the beaten egg in a circular movement so that it cooks in threads in the soup.

5 Adjust the seasoning and serve each portion topped with a whole prawn (shrimp).

Spinach & Tofu Soup

Tofu (bean curd) is very popular with vegetarians, being a good source of protein.

SERVES 4

125–175 g/ 4–6 oz fresh spinach leaves,
or frozen leaf spinach, defrosted
small bunch of chives • 2 tbsp sesame oil
1 garlic clove, crushed
125–175 g/ 4–6 oz tofu (bean curd),
cut into 1 cm/ ½ inch cubes
60 g/ 2 oz/ ½ cup pine kernels
1 litre/ 1¾ pints/ 4 cups chicken or vegetable stock
½ tsp turmeric • ½ tsp ground coriander
2 tsp cornflour (cornstarch) • salt and pepper

1 Rinse the spinach thoroughly and remove the stalks. Dry on paper towels, then slice into thin strips. If using frozen spinach, drain well, then slice or chop roughly.

2 Take 12 chives and tie 3 at a time into a knot to use for a garnish, if liked. Chop the remainder.

3 Heat the oil in a wok, swirling it around until really hot. Add the garlic and tofu and stir-fry for 2–3 minutes until they are beginning to colour. Add the pine kernels and continue to cook until they turn a light golden brown. Add the stock, turmeric, coriander and seasoning and bring to the boil; simmer for 10 minutes.

4 Blend the cornflour (cornstarch) with a little cold water and stir into the wok. Add the strips of spinach and simmer for a further 2–3 minutes, stirring frequently.

5 Adjust the seasoning, stir in the snipped chives and garnish each serving with a chive knot, if liked.

Wonton Soup

Filled wontons are served in a clear soup.

SERVES 4

Wonton skins:
1 egg • 6 tbsp water
250 g/8 oz/2 cups plain (all-purpose) flour

Filling:
125 g/4 oz/½ cup frozen chopped spinach, defrosted
15 g/½ oz/1 tbsp pine kernels (nuts), toasted and chopped
30 g/1 oz/¼ cup minced quorn (TVP) • salt

Soup:
600 ml/1 pint/2½ cups vegetable stock
1 tbsp dry sherry • 1 tbsp light soy sauce
2 spring onions (scallions), chopped

1 Beat the egg lightly in a bowl and mix with the water. Stir in the flour to form a stiff dough. Knead lightly, then cover with a damp cloth and leave to rest for 30 minutes. Roll the dough out into a large sheet about 5 mm/¼ inch thick. Cut out 24 × 7.5 cm/3 inch squares. Dust each one lightly with flour. Only 12 squares are required for the soup so freeze the remainder.

2 To make the filling, squeeze out the excess water from the spinach. Mix the spinach with the pine kernels (nuts) and quorn (TVP). Season with salt. Divide the mixture into 12 equal portions and place one portion in the centre of each square. Bring the opposite corners of the square together and squeeze to seal.

3 To make the soup, bring the stock, sherry and soy sauce to the boil, add the wontons and boil rapidly for 2–3 minutes. Add the spring onions (scallions) and serve in warmed soup bowls.

Hot & Sour Soup

This is the most popular soup in Chinese restaurants and homes throughout the world.

SERVES 4

*4–6 dried Chinese mushrooms, soaked in warm water
for 30 minutes
125 g/ 4 oz cooked pork or chicken
1 cake tofu (bean curd)
60 g/2 oz canned sliced bamboo shoots, drained
600 ml/ 1 pint/ 2½ cups Chinese Stock (see page 24) or water
1 tbsp Chinese rice wine or dry sherry
1 tbsp light soy sauce
2 tbsp rice vinegar
salt and pepper
2–3 spring onions (scallions), sliced thinly, to serve*

Cornflour (cornstarch) paste:
1 tbsp cornflour (cornstarch) • 1½ tbsp cold water

1 Drain the mushrooms, squeeze dry and discard the hard stalks. Thinly slice the mushrooms.

2 Thinly slice the meat, tofu (bean curd) and bamboo shoots into narrow shreds.

3 Make the cornflour (cornstarch) paste: blend the cornflour (cornstarch) with the water in a bowl until smooth.

4 Bring the stock or water to a rolling boil in a wok or large pan and add the mushrooms, meat, tofu (bean curd) and bamboo shoots. Return to the boil and simmer for about 1 minute. Add the wine, soy sauce, vinegar, salt and pepper. Bring back to the boil once more, stirring in the cornflour (cornstarch) paste to thicken the soup. Serve hot, sprinkled with the spring onions (scallions).

Three-Flavour Soup

**If raw prawns (shrimp) are not available,
add ready-cooked ones at the last stage.
Left-over Chinese Stock can be kept in the
refrigerator for 4–5 days or frozen.**

SERVES 4

*125 g/4 oz boned and skinned chicken breast
125 g/4 oz raw peeled prawns (shrimp)
½ egg white, beaten lightly
2 tsp Cornflour (Cornstarch) Paste (see page 22)
125 g/4 oz honey-roast ham • salt and pepper
finely chopped spring onions (scallions), to garnish*

Chinese stock (makes 2.5 l/4 pints/10 cups):
*750 g/1½ lb chicken pieces • 750 g/1½ lb pork spare ribs
3.75 litres/6 pints/15 cups cold water
3–4 pieces of ginger root, crushed
3–4 spring onions (scallions), each tied into a knot
3–4 tbsp Chinese rice wine or dry sherry*

1 Slice the chicken into thin shreds. If the prawns (shrimp) are large, cut each in half lengthways, otherwise leave whole. Place the chicken and prawns (shrimps) in a bowl and mix with a pinch of salt, the egg white and cornflour (cornstarch) paste until well coated.

2 Cut the ham into thin slices roughly the same size as the chicken pieces.

3 To make the Chinese Stock, trim off the excess fat from the chicken and spare ribs and chop into large pieces. Place the meat in a large pan with the water and add the ginger and spring onion (scallion) knots. Bring to the boil, and skim off the scum. Reduce the heat and simmer uncovered for 2–3 hours. Strain the stock through a collander, discarding the chicken, pork, ginger and spring onions

(scallions). Return the stock to the pan. Add the wine and simmer for 2–3 minutes.

raw prawns (shrimps) and the ham. Bring back to the boil, and simmer for 1 minute.

4 Put 750 ml/1¼ pints/ 3 cups stock or water in a pan and bring to a rolling boil. Add the chicken, the

5 Season with salt and pepper and serve the soup hot, garnished with the spring onions (scallions).

Pork & Szechuan Vegetable Soup

Sold in cans, Szechuan preserved vegetable is pickled mustard root which is quite hot and salty, so rinse in water before use.

SERVES 4

250 g/ 8 oz pork fillet
2 tsp Cornflour (Cornstarch) Paste (see page 22)
125 g/ 4 oz Szechuan preserved vegetable
750 ml/ 1¼ pints/ 3 cups Chinese Stock (see page 24)
or water
salt and pepper
a few drops of sesame oil (optional)
2–3 spring onions (scallions), sliced, to garnish

1 Cut the pork across the grain into thin shreds and mix with the cornflour (cornstarch) paste.

2 Wash and rinse the Szechuan preserved vegetable, then cut into thin shreds about the same size as the pork.

3 Bring the stock or water to a rolling boil in a wok or pan. Add the pork, stir to separate the shreds and bring back to the boil.

4 Add the Szechuan preserved vegetable and bring back to the boil once more. Season with salt and pepper and sprinkle with sesame oil (if using). Serve hot, garnished with spring onions (scallions).

Spring Rolls

Spring roll wrappers are available from oriental shops and some supermarkets.

MAKES 12

5 Chinese dried mushrooms (or open-cup mushrooms)
1 large carrot • 60 g/2 oz/1 cup canned bamboo shoots
2 spring onions (scallions) • 60 g/2 oz Chinese leaves
2 tbsp vegetable oil • 250 g/8 oz/4 cups bean-sprouts
1 tbsp soy sauce • 12 spring roll wrappers
1 egg, beaten • vegetable oil for deep-frying • salt

1 Place the mushrooms in a small bowl and cover with warm water. Leave to soak for 20–25 minutes. Drain the mushrooms and squeeze out the excess water. Remove the tough centres and slice the mushrooms fairly thinly. Cut the carrot and bamboo shoots into very thin julienne strips. Chop the spring onions (scallions) and shred the Chinese leaves.

2 Heat the 2 tablespoons of oil in a wok or frying pan (skillet). Add the mushrooms, carrot and bamboo shoots, and stir-fry for 2 minutes. Add the spring onions (scallions), Chinese leaves, bean-sprouts and soy sauce. Season with salt and stir-fry for 2 minutes. Leave to cool.

Divide the mixture into 12 equal portions and place one portion on the edge of each spring roll wrapper. Fold in the sides and roll each one up, brushing the join with a little beaten egg to seal.

3 Heat the oil in a wok or large saucepan to 180–190°C/350–375°F or until a cube of bread browns in 30 seconds. Deep-fry the spring rolls in batches for 4–5 minutes, until golden and crispy. If the oil is too hot the rolls will brown on the outside before cooking on the inside. Remove and drain on paper towels. Keep each batch of rolls warm while the others are being cooked. Serve at once.

Money Bags

Try dipping these steamed dumplings in a mixture of soy sauce, sherry and slivers of ginger root.

SERVES 4

3 Chinese dried mushrooms (or thinly sliced open-cup mushrooms)
250 g/ 8 oz/ 2 cups plain (all-purpose) flour
1 egg, beaten • 75 ml/ 3 fl oz/ ⅓ cup water
1 tsp baking powder • ¾ tsp salt
2 tbsp vegetable oil • 2 spring onions (scallions), chopped
90 g/ 3 oz/ ½ cup sweetcorn kernels
½ red chilli, deseeded and chopped
1 tbsp brown bean sauce

1 Place the dried mushrooms in a small bowl, cover with warm water and leave to soak for 20–25 minutes. Remove the tough centres and chop the mushrooms.

2 To make the wrappers, sift the flour into a bowl. Add the egg and mix lightly. Stir in the water, baking powder and salt. Mix to a soft dough. Knead lightly until smooth on a floured board. Cover with a damp cloth and set aside for 5–6 minutes. This allows the baking powder time to activate, so that the dumplings swell when they are steamed.

3 Drain the mushrooms, squeezing them dry.

4 Heat the oil in a wok or large frying pan (skillet) and stir-fry the mushrooms, spring onions (scallions), sweetcorn and chilli for 2 minutes. Stir in the brown bean sauce and remove from the heat.

5 Roll the dough into a large sausage and cut into 24 even-sized pieces. Roll each piece out into a thin round and place a teaspoonful of the filling in the centre. Gather up the edges, pinch together and twist to seal.

6 Stand the dumplings in an oiled bamboo steamer. Place over a saucepan of simmering water, cover and steam for 12–14 minutes before serving.

Pork & Prawn (Shrimp) Sesame Toasts

This classic Thai snack is a great nibble for serving at parties.

SERVES 4

250 g/ 8 oz lean pork
250 g/ 8 oz/²⁄₃ cup uncooked peeled prawns (shrimp), deveined
4 spring onions (scallions), trimmed • 1 garlic clove, crushed
1 tbsp chopped fresh coriander (cilantro) leaves and stems
1 tbsp fish sauce • 1 egg
8–10 slices of thick-cut white bread
3 tbsp sesame seeds • 150 ml/¼ pint/²⁄₃ cup vegetable oil
salt and pepper

To garnish:
sprigs of fresh coriander (cilantro)
red (bell) pepper, sliced finely

1 Put the pork, prawns (shrimp), spring onions (scallions), garlic, coriander (cilantro), fish sauce, egg and seasoning into a food processor or blender. Process for a few seconds to chop the ingredients finely. Transfer the mixture to a bowl. Alternatively, chop the pork, prawns (shrimp) and spring onions (scallions) very finely, and mix with the garlic, coriander (cilantro), fish sauce, beaten egg and seasoning until well combined.

2 Spread the pork and prawn (shrimp) mixture thickly over the bread so that it reaches to the edges. Cut off the crusts and cut each slice of bread into 4 pieces. Sprinkle the topping liberally with sesame seeds.

3 Heat the oil in a wok or frying pan (skillet). Fry a few pieces of the bread, topping side down first so that it sets the egg, for about 2 minutes or until golden brown. Turn the pieces over

and cook the other side for about 1 minute. Remove the pork and prawn (shrimp) toasts with a slotted spoon and drain them on paper towels. Fry the remaining pieces in batches until they are all cooked.

4 Serve garnished with sprigs of fresh coriander (cilantro) and (bell) pepper.

Little Golden Parcels

These simply prepared little parcels will draw admiring gasps from your guests.

MAKES 30

1 garlic clove, crushed
1 tsp chopped coriander (cilantro) root • 1 tsp pepper
250 g/8 oz boiled mashed potato
175 g/6 oz/1 cup water chestnuts, chopped finely
1 tsp grated ginger root • 2 tbsp ground roast peanuts
2 tsp light soy sauce • ½ tsp salt
½ tsp sugar • 30 wonton sheets, defrosted
1 tsp cornflour (cornstarch), made into a paste
with 1 tbsp cold water
vegetable oil, for deep-frying • fresh chives, to garnish
sweet chilli sauce, to serve

1 Combine all the ingredients thoroughly, except the wonton sheets, cornflour (cornstarch) paste and oil.

2 Lay 4 wonton sheets out on a work surface (counter), keeping the remaining sheets covered with a damp cloth. Put a teaspoonful of the mixture on each wonton sheet. Drizzle a line of the cornflour (cornstarch) paste around each sheet, about 1 cm/½ inch from the edges.

3 Bring all 4 corners to the centre of each sheet and press together to form a little bags. Continue the process of filling and wrapping until all the wonton sheets are used.

4 Meanwhile, heat 5 cm/ 2 inches of the vegetable oil in a deep saucepan until a light haze appears on top. Lower in the parcels, in batches of 3. Fry until golden brown, then remove with a slotted spoon and leave to drain on paper towels.

5 Tie a chive around the neck of each bag to garnish, and serve with a sweet chilli sauce for dipping.

Fat Horses

This classic Thai snack is a great nibble for parties – but be sure to make plenty!

SERVES 4

30 g/ 1 oz/ 2 tbsp creamed coconut • 125 g/ 4 oz lean pork
125 g/ 4 oz chicken breast, skin removed
125 g/ 4 oz/ ½ cup canned crab meat, drained
2 eggs • 2 garlic cloves, crushed
4 spring onions (scallions), trimmed and chopped
1 tbsp fish sauce
1 tbsp chopped fresh coriander (cilantro) leaves and stems
1 tbsp dark muscovado sugar • salt and pepper

To garnish:
finely sliced white radish (mooli) or turnip • chives
red chilli • sprigs of fresh coriander (cilantro)

1 Put the coconut into a bowl and pour over 3 tablespoons of hot water. Stir to dissolve the coconut.

2 Put the pork, chicken and crab meat into a food processor or blender and process for 10–15 seconds until minced (ground), or chop them finely by hand and put in a mixing bowl. Add the coconut mixture to the food processor or blender with the eggs, garlic, spring onions (scallions), fish sauce, coriander (cilantro) and sugar. Season with salt and pepper and process for a few more seconds. Alternatively, mix these ingredients into the chopped meat.

3 Grease 6 ramekin dishes with a little butter. Spoon in the minced (ground) mixture, levelling the surface. Place them in a steamer, then set the steamer over a pan of gently boiling water. Cook until set – about 30 minutes. Lift out the dishes and leave to cool for a few minutes. Run a knife around the edge of each dish, then invert on to warmed plates to serve.

Samosas

Each filling recipe makes enough to fill all the pastry.

MAKES 32

Pastry:

500 g/1 lb 2 oz/4 cups plain (all-purpose) flour
½ tsp turmeric • ½ tsp salt
100 g/3½ oz/scant ½ cup ghee
about 200 ml/7 fl oz/¾ cup milk, mixed with a little
lemon juice

Tuna filling:

½ tsp each of turmeric and cayenne • 1 tsp ground cumin
1 tsp ground coriander • 200 g/7 oz can of tuna, drained
60 g/2 oz/⅓ cup frozen peas, cooked
60 g/2 oz/½ cup boiled potatoes, diced • salt and pepper

Vegetarian filling:

250 g/8 oz white potatoes, boiled
½ × 400 g/14 oz can of artichoke hearts, drained and puréed
1 tsp ground black pepper • 2 tsp coriander seeds, ground
1 tsp cumin seeds, ground • ½ tsp fenugreek seeds, ground
2 large tomatoes, peeled and deseeded
90 g/3 oz/½ cup frozen peas, cooked • salt and pepper

Sauce:

6 anchovies • 2 tbsp natural yogurt • salt and pepper

1 To make the tuna filling, roast the spices in a large frying pan (skillet). Remove from the heat and add the tuna, peas and potatoes. Stir well and season. Continue from step 3.

2 To make the vegetarian filling, mash the potatoes and combine with the artichokes. Roast the spices in a large frying pan (skillet). Remove from the heat and add the potato mixture. Stir

well to combine. Chop the
tomatoes and carefully fold in
with the peas. Season.

3 Roll out the pastry and
cut out 16 × 12 cm/
5 inch circles. Cut each circle
in half and put a teaspoonful
of filling on each half. Brush
the edges with the milk and

lemon and fold each half over
to form a triangle. Seal well,
and crimp the edges. Bake in
a preheated oven at 190°C/
375°F/Gas mark 5.

4 To make the sauce, mash
the anchovies, mix with
the yogurt and season. Serve
with the hot samosas.

Spicy Bites

Here are three delicious morsels to whet your appetite before a meal. Use courgettes (zucchini) with the flowers still attached.

SERVES 4

Spiced nuts:

125 g/ 4 oz/ 1 cup mixed nuts, such as peanuts, cashews and blanched almonds • 1 dried red chilli
1 tsp sunflower oil • 1 garlic clove • ½ tsp salt
1 tsp Garam Masala (see page 9) • ½ tsp clear honey

Deep-fried courgettes (zucchini):

125 g/ 4 oz/ 1 cup plain (all-purpose) flour
½ tsp each turmeric and cayenne pepper
150 ml/ ¼ pint/ ⅔ cup water • 2 eggs
vegetable oil • 1 courgette (zucchini), cut into batons

Mussel morsels:

1 kg/ 2 lb small mussels, scrubbed
3 tbsp mayonnaise • 1 tsp Garam Masala (see page 9)
½ red chilli, deseeded and chopped finely
2 spring onions (scallions), chopped finely
45 g/ 1½ oz/ ¾ cup white breadcrumbs • salt

Spiced Nuts

1 Cook the nuts in a dry, heavy-based pan over a moderate heat until the oil is released, about 5 minutes. Add the remaining ingredients except the honey, and cook for 3 minutes, stirring. Add the honey and cook for 2 minutes. Remove from heat and turn into a serving dish.

Deep-Fried Courgettes (Zucchini)

1 Sift the flour and spices together. Add the water, eggs and 1 tablespoon of oil. Whisk until smooth. Heat a little oil in a wok. Dip the batons into the batter, and carefully drop into the oil. When cooked, remove and drain on paper towels.

Mussel Morsels

1 Put a little water into a large pan. Discard any mussels that are not closed. Add the mussels and cover the pan. Cook over a high heat for 5 minutes; do not uncover. Drain the mussels and discard any unopened ones. Remove the shells and reserve them. Chop the mussel meat finely. Stir the mayonnaise into the mussel meat. Add the remaining ingredients and season to taste. Spoon the mixture back into the shells, and arrange on a serving plate.

Indian Prawns (Shrimp)

These prawns (shrimp) look stunning when presented on the skewers, and make an impressive prelude to a meal.

SERVES 4

8 wooden skewers
500 g/ 1 lb 2 oz or 16 raw tiger prawns (shrimp), shelled, leaving tails intact
juice of 2 limes • 1 tsp cardamom seeds
2 tsp cumin seeds, ground
2 tsp coriander seeds, ground
½ tsp ground cinnamon • 1 tsp ground turmeric
1 tsp cayenne pepper • 1 garlic clove, crushed
2 tbsp oil • cucumber slices, to garnish

1 Soak 8 wooden skewers in water for 20 minutes to prevent them from scorching. Cut the prawns (shrimp) lengthways in half down to the tail, so that they flatten out to a symmetrical shape.

2 Thread a prawn (shrimp) on to 2 wooden skewers, with the tail between them, so that the skewers hold the prawn (shrimp) in shape. Thread another 3 prawns (shrimp) on to these 2 skewers in the same way. Repeat with the remaining prawns (shrimp) and skewers until you have 4 sets of 4 prawns (shrimps) each.

3 Lay the skewered prawns (shrimp) in a non-porous, non-metallic dish, and sprinkle over the lime juice.

4 Mix the spices, garlic and oil, and coat the prawns (shrimp) in the mixture. Cover and chill for 4 hours.

5 Cook over a hot barbecue or in a grill (broiler) pan lined with foil under a preheated grill (broiler) for 6 minutes, turning once.

6 Serve immediately, garnished with cucumber slices and accompanied by a sweet chutney.

Prawns (Shrimp) in Sauce

**Use raw tiger prawns (shrimp) with the
shell removed and just the tail left in place.**

SERVES 4

20–24 large raw tiger prawns (shrimp)
45 g/ 1½ oz/ ½ cup desiccated (shredded) coconut
90 g/ 3 oz/ 1¼ cups fresh white breadcrumbs
1 egg, beaten
600 ml/ 1 pint/ 2½ cups sunflower or vegetable oil
½ small honeydew or Ogen melon
fresh sprigs of coriander (cilantro), to garnish

Peanut & coconut sauce:
60 g/ 2 oz creamed coconut
150 ml/ ¼ pint/ ⅔ cup hot water
125 g/ 4 oz crunchy peanut butter
2 spring onions (scallions), trimmed and finely chopped
1 tbsp dark soy sauce • 1 tsp brown sugar
2 tsp sesame seeds • salt and pepper

1 Peel the tiger prawns (shrimp), leaving the tails, and dry on paper towels. Put the coconut and breadcrumbs into a food processor and process until finely blended and chopped. Spread on a plate. Dip the prawns (shrimp) in the beaten egg, then coat in the coconut and breadcrumb mixture. Chill while making the sauce.

2 For the sauce, put the creamed coconut and water into the wok and blend thoroughly, then bring slowly to the boil. Remove from the heat, stir in the peanut butter, spring onions (scallions), soy sauce, sugar, sesame seeds and seasoning and when blended put into a serving bowl and keep warm.

3 Cut the melon into 12 slices, removing the seeds.

4 Wash and dry the wok, add the oil and heat to

180°–190°C/350°–375°F, or until a cube of bread browns in 30 seconds. Deep-fry the prawns (shrimp) a few at a time for 2–3 minutes until golden brown. Remove with a slotted spoon and drain on paper towels.

Keep warm while cooking the remainder.

5 Serve on individual plates with slices of melon, garnished with sprigs of coriander (cilantro). Serve the warm sauce separately.

Butterfly Prawns (Shrimp)

Use unpeeled, raw king or tiger prawns (jumbo shrimp) which are about 7–10 cm (3–4 inches) long.

SERVES 4

12 raw tiger prawns (jumbo shrimp) in their shells
2 tbsp light soy sauce
1 tbsp Chinese rice wine or dry sherry
1 tbsp cornflour (cornstarch)
vegetable oil for deep-frying
2 eggs, lightly beaten
8–10 tbsp breadcrumbs
salt and pepper
shredded lettuce leaves, to serve
chopped spring onions (scallions), to garnish

1 Shell and devein the prawns (shrimp) but leave the tails on. Split them in half from the underbelly about halfway along, leaving the tails still firmly attached.

2 Mix together the soy sauce, wine, cornflour (cornstarch), and salt and pepper in a bowl, add the prawns (shrimp) and turn to coat. Leave to marinate for 10–15 minutes.

3 Heat the oil in a preheated wok to 180–190°C/350–375°F or until a cube of bread browns in 30 seconds. Pick up each prawn (shrimp) by the tail, dip it in the beaten egg then roll it in the breadcrumbs to coat well.

4 Deep-fry the prawns (shrimp) in batches until golden brown. Remove with a slotted spoon and drain on paper towels.

5 To serve, arrange the prawns (shrimp) on a bed of lettuce leaves and garnish with spring onions (scallions), either raw or soaked in a tablespoon of the hot oil for about 30 seconds.

Poultry & Meat

Chicken is probably one of the
most frequently used meats in
Indian cooking. Muslims do not
eat anything derived from the
pig for religious reasons, as it is
considered unclean, while
Hindus are largely vegetarian.
Meat, of all types, also makes
for a varied cuisine in China
and Thailand.

Chicken Jalfrezi

This is a quick and tasty way to use leftover roast chicken. The sauce can also be used for any cooked poultry, lamb or beef.

SERVES 4

1 tsp mustard oil • 3 tbsp vegetable oil
1 large onion, chopped finely • 3 garlic cloves, crushed
1 tbsp tomato purée (paste)
2 tomatoes, skinned and chopped
1 tsp ground turmeric
½ tsp cumin seeds, ground
½ tsp coriander seeds, ground
½ tsp chilli powder • ½ tsp Garam Masala (see page 9)
1 tsp red wine vinegar
1 small red (bell) pepper, chopped
125 g/ 4 oz/ 1 cup frozen broad (fava) beans
500 g/ 1 lb 2 oz cooked chicken, cut into bite-sized pieces
salt • sprigs of fresh coriander (cilantro), to garnish
cooked rice, to serve

1 Heat the mustard oil in a large frying pan (skillet) set over a high heat for 1 minute until it begins to smoke. Add the vegetable oil, reduce the heat and then add the onion and garlic. Fry the garlic and onion until golden.

2 Add the tomato purée (paste), chopped tomatoes, turmeric, ground cumin and coriander seeds, chilli powder, garam masala and vinegar to the frying pan (skillet). Stir the mixture until fragrant.

3 Add the red (bell) pepper and broad (fava) beans and stir for 2 minutes until the pepper is softened. Stir in the chicken, and salt to taste. Simmer gently for 6–8 minutes until the chicken is heated through and the beans are tender. Garnish with coriander (cilantro) sprigs and serve with cooked rice.

Tandoori Chicken

To replicate the traditional tandoor oven, cook this chicken at a very high temperature, preferably on a barbecue.

SERVES 4

*8 small chicken pieces, skinned • 3 dried red chillies
1 tsp salt • 2 tsp coriander seeds
2 tbsp lime juice • 2 garlic cloves, crushed
2.5 cm/ 1 inch piece of ginger root, grated • 1 clove
2 tsp Garam Masala (see page 9) • 2 tsp chilli powder
½ onion, chopped
300 ml/½ pint/ 1¼ cups natural yogurt
1 tbsp chopped fresh coriander (cilantro)
lemon slices, to garnish
Cucumber Raita (see page 9), to serve*

1 Make 2–3 slashes with a sharp knife in the flesh of the chicken pieces.

2 Crush together the chillies, salt, coriander seeds, lime juice, garlic, ginger and clove. Stir in the garam masala and chilli powder. Transfer to a small saucepan and heat gently until aromatic. Add the onion and fry. Stir in the yogurt and remove the pan from the heat.

3 Arrange the chicken in a non-metallic dish and pour over the yogurt mixture. Cover and leave in the refrigerator to marinate for 4 hours or overnight.

4 Arrange the chicken on a grill (broiler) tray and cook under a preheated very hot grill (broiler) or over a barbecue for 20–30 minutes, turning once, until the chicken juices run clear when the thickest parts of the portions are pierced with a sharp knife.

5 Sprinkle the chicken with chopped fresh coriander (cilantro). Serve hot or cold, garnished with the lemon slices and accompanied by cucumber raita.

Chicken Tikka Masala

**Serve this rich dish with accompaniments
to provide a balance to the fiery flavours.**

SERVES 4

8 skewers • ½ onion, chopped coarsely
60 g/2 oz/4 tbsp tomato purée (paste) • 1 tsp cumin seeds
2.5 cm/1 inch piece of ginger root, chopped
3 tbsp lemon juice • 2 garlic cloves, crushed
2 tsp chilli powder • 750 g/1½ lb boneless chicken
salt and pepper • sprigs of fresh mint, to garnish

Masala sauce:
2 tbsp ghee • 1 onion, sliced
1 tbsp black onion seeds • 3 garlic cloves, crushed
2 fresh green chillies, chopped
200 g/7 oz can tomatoes
120 ml/4 fl oz/½ cup natural yogurt
120 ml/4 fl oz/½ cup coconut milk
1 tbsp chopped fresh coriander (cilantro)
1 tbsp chopped fresh mint • 2 tbsp lemon or lime juice
½ tsp Garam Masala (see page 9) • vegetable oil

1 Purée the onion, tomato purée (paste), cumin, ginger, lemon juice, garlic, chilli powder, salt and pepper in a blender and transfer to a bowl. Alternatively, grind the cumin with a pestle and mortar and transfer to a bowl. Chop the onion and ginger and stir into the bowl with the tomato purée (paste), lemon juice, salt and pepper, garlic and chilli powder.

2 Cut chicken into 5 cm/2 inch cubes. Stir into the spiced mixture and leave to marinate for 2 hours.

3 Make the masala sauce. Heat the ghee in a large saucepan, add the onion and stir over a medium heat for 5 minutes. Add the onion seeds, garlic and chillies and cook until aromatic. Add the tomatoes, yogurt and

coconut milk, and simmer for 20 minutes.

4 Meanwhile, divide the marinated chicken evenly between 8 oiled skewers and cook under a preheated very hot grill (broiler) for 15 minutes, turning frequently. Remove the chicken from the skewers and add to the masala sauce. Stir in the coriander (cilantro), mint, lemon or lime juice, and garam masala. Serve garnished with sprigs of mint.

Chicken with Peanut Sauce

A tangy stir-fry with a strong peanut flavour. Serve with freshly boiled rice or noodles.

SERVES 4

4 boneless, skinned chicken breasts, about 625 g/1¼ lb
4 tbsp soy sauce • 4 tbsp sherry
3 tbsp crunchy peanut butter
350 g/12 oz courgettes (zucchini), trimmed
2 tbsp sunflower oil
4–6 spring onions (scallions), thinly sliced diagonally
1 × 250 g/8 oz can of bamboo shoots, drained and sliced
salt and pepper • 4 tbsp desiccated (shredded) coconut, toasted

1 Cut the chicken into thin strips across the grain and season lightly with salt and pepper.

2 Mix the soy sauce in a bowl with the sherry and peanut butter until smooth and well blended.

3 Cut the courgettes (zucchini) into 5 cm/ 2 inch lengths and then cut into sticks about 5 mm/ ¼ inch thick.

4 Heat the oil in the wok, swirling it around until it is really hot. Add the spring onions (scallions) and stir-fry for 1–2 minutes, then add the chicken and stir-fry for 3–4 minutes until well sealed and almost cooked.

5 Add the courgettes (zucchini) and bamboo shoots and continue to stir-fry for 1–2 minutes.

6 Add the peanut butter mixture and heat thoroughly, stirring all the time so everything is coated in the sauce as it thickens. Adjust the seasoning and serve very hot, sprinkled with toasted coconut.

Kung Po Chicken with Cashew Nuts

Peanuts, walnuts or almonds can be used instead of the cashew nuts, if preferred.

SERVES 4

250–300 g/ 8–10 oz boned and skinned chicken meat
¼ tsp salt
⅓ egg white
1 tsp Cornflour (Cornstarch) Paste (see page 22)
1 green (bell) pepper, cored and deseeded
4 tbsp vegetable oil
1 spring onion (scallion), cut into short sections
a few small slices of ginger root
4–5 small dried red chillies, soaked, deseeded and shredded
2 tbsp crushed yellow bean sauce
1 tsp rice wine or dry sherry
125 g/ 4 oz roasted cashew nuts
a few drops of sesame oil • boiled rice, to serve

1 Cut the chicken into small cubes about the size of sugar lumps. Place in a small bowl and mix with a pinch of salt, the egg white and the cornflour (cornstarch) paste, in that order. Cut the green (bell) pepper into cubes or triangles about the same size as the chicken pieces.

2 Heat the oil in a preheated wok, add the chicken cubes and stir-fry for about 1 minute, or until the colour changes. Remove the chicken with a slotted spoon and keep warm.

3 Add the spring onion (scallion), ginger, chillies and green (bell) pepper to the wok. Stir-fry for about 1 minute, then add the chicken with the yellow bean sauce and wine. Blend well and stir-fry for 1 minute. Finally stir in the cashew nuts and sesame oil. Serve hot, with boiled rice.

Bang-Bang Chicken

The cooked chicken meat is tenderized by beating with a rolling pin, hence the name for this very popular Szechuan dish.

SERVES 4

1 litre/ 1¾ pints/ 4 cups water
2 chicken quarters (breast half and leg)
1 cucumber, cut into matchsticks

Sauce:
2 tbsp light soy sauce
1 tsp sugar
1 tbsp finely chopped spring onions (scallions)
1 tsp red chilli oil
¼ tsp pepper
1 tsp white sesame seeds
2 tbsp peanut butter, creamed with a little sesame oil

1 Bring the water to a rolling boil in a wok or a large pan. Add the chicken pieces, reduce the heat, cover and cook for 30–35 minutes.

2 Remove the chicken from the pan and immerse in a bowl of cold water for at least 1 hour to cool, ready for shredding.

3 Remove the chicken pieces and drain well. Pat dry with paper towels, then take the meat off the bone.

4 On a flat surface, pound the chicken with a rolling pin, then tear the meat into even-sized shreds with 2 forks. Mix the chicken with the shredded cucumber and arrange in a shallow serving dish.

5 To serve, mix together all the sauce ingredients and pour over the chicken.

Lemon Chicken

Lemon sauce is a Cantonese speciality, easily available from oriental stores, or you can make your own.

SERVES 4

350 g/12 oz boned and skinned chicken breasts
1 tbsp rice wine or dry sherry
1 egg, beaten
4 tbsp plain (all-purpose) flour blended with 2 tbsp water
vegetable oil for deep-frying
salt and pepper
slices of fresh lemon, to garnish • boiled rice, to serve

Lemon sauce:
1 tbsp vegetable oil
250 ml/8 fl oz/1 cup Chinese Stock (see page 24) or water
1 tbsp caster sugar • 1 tbsp lemon juice
1 tbsp cornflour (cornstarch)
1 tsp salt • 1 tsp lemon rind

1 To make the lemon sauce, heat the oil in a wok until hot, reduce the heat and add all the other ingredients. Blend well, then boil and stir until smooth.

2 Cut the chicken into thin slices and place in a dish with wine, and salt and pepper. Leave to marinate for 25–30 minutes. Make a batter with the egg and the flour paste. Place the chicken slices in the batter and coat well.

3 Heat the oil in a wok or deep-fryer to 180–190°C/350–375°F or until a cube for bread browns in 30 seconds. Deep-fry the chicken until golden, remove and drain on paper towels. Cut the chicken slices into bite-sized pieces.

4 Heat 1 tablespoon of oil in a wok or pan. Stir in the lemon sauce until blended and pour over the chicken. Garnish with lemon slices.

Red Chicken Curry

The curry paste is fiery hot – for a milder version, reduce the number of chillies used.

SERVES 6

4 tbsp vegetable oil • 2 garlic cloves, crushed
400 ml/ 14 fl oz/ 1¾ cups coconut milk
6 chicken breast fillets, skinned and cut into bite-sized pieces
125 ml/ 4 fl oz/ ½ cup chicken stock • 2 tbsp fish sauce
3 tbsp thick coconut milk or cream
finely chopped chillies, lemon grass and lemon slices, to garnish
cooked rice, to serve

Red curry paste:
8 dried red chillies, deseeded and chopped
2.5 cm/ 1 inch piece of galangal or ginger root, peeled and sliced
3 stalks lemon grass, chopped • 1 garlic clove, peeled
2 tsp shrimp paste • 1 kaffir lime leaf, chopped
1 tsp ground coriander (cilantro) • ¾ tsp ground cumin
1 tbsp chopped fresh coriander • 1 tsp salt • 1 tsp black pepper

1 To make the curry paste, put all the ingredients in a food processor or blender and process until smooth.

2 Heat the oil in a large, heavy-based pan or wok. Add the garlic and cook for 1 minute or until golden. Stir in the curry paste and cook for 10–15 seconds then gradually add the coconut milk, stirring constantly (don't worry if the mixture starts to look curdled at this stage).

Add the chicken pieces and turn in the sauce mixture to coat. Cook gently for about 3–5 minutes or until almost tender. Stir in the chicken stock and fish sauce, mixing well, then cook for 2 minutes.

3 Transfer the chicken to a warmed dish. To serve, spoon on a little of the thick coconut milk or cream and garnish with chopped chillies, lemon grass and lemon slices. Serve with rice.

Green Chilli Chicken

**The chilli paste gives a hot, spicy flavour
and vibrant green colour to the chicken.**

SERVES 4

5 tbsp vegetable oil
500 g/1 lb 2 oz boneless chicken breasts, sliced into thin strips
50 ml/2 fl oz/¼ cup coconut milk • 3 tbsp brown sugar
3 tsp fish sauce • 3 tbsp sliced red and green chillies, deseeded
4–6 tbsp chopped fresh basil
*Kaffir lime leaves, sliced red chillies and chopped coriander
(cilantro), to garnish*

Green curry paste:

2 tsp ground ginger • 2 tsp ground coriander
2 tsp caraway seeds • 2 tsp ground nutmeg
2 tsp shrimp paste • 2 tsp salt
2 tsp black pepper • pinch of ground cloves
1 stalk lemon grass, finely chopped
2 tbsp chopped coriander • 2 garlic cloves, peeled

1 To make the curry paste, place all the ingredients and 2 tablespoons of the oil in a food processor or blender and process to a smooth paste.

2 Heat the remaining oil in a heavy-based pan or wok. Add the curry paste and cook for about 30 seconds. Add the chicken strips to the wok and stir-fry over a high heat for about 2–3 minutes.

Add the coconut milk, brown sugar, fish sauce and chillies. Cook for 5 minutes, stirring.

3 Remove from the heat, add the basil and toss well to mix.

4 Transfer the chicken to a warmed serving dish and garnish with lime leaves, sliced red chillies and chopped coriander (cilantro). Serve with rice.

Peanut Sesame Chicken

A quick to make chicken and vegetable dish. Sesame and peanuts give it crunch and the fruit juice glaze gives a lovely shiny coating to the sauce.

SERVES 4

2 tbsp vegetable oil
2 tbsp sesame oil
500 g/ 1 lb 2 oz boned and skinned chicken breasts, sliced into strips
250 g/ 8 oz broccoli, divided into small florets
250 g/ 8 oz baby sweetcorn cobs
1 small red (bell) pepper, cored, deseeded and sliced
2 tbsp soy sauce
250 ml/ 8 fl oz/ 1 cup orange juice
2 tsp cornflour (cornstarch)
2 tbsp toasted sesame seeds
60 g/ 2 oz/ ⅓ cup roasted, shelled, unsalted peanuts
rice or noodles, to serve

1 Heat the oils in a large, heavy-based frying pan (skillet) or wok, add the chicken strips and stir-fry until browned, about 4–5 minutes.

2 Add the broccoli, sweetcorn cobs and red (bell) pepper and stir-fry for 1–2 minutes.

3 Meanwhile, mix the soy sauce with the orange juice and cornflour (cornstarch). Stir into the chicken and vegetable mixture, stirring constantly until the sauce has slightly thickened and a glaze develops.

4 Stir in the sesame seeds and peanuts, mixing well. Heat for 3–4 minutes. Serve at once, with rice or noodles.

Duck with Ginger & Lime

**Just the thing for a lazy summer day –
slices of roasted duck breasts on a bed of
assorted fresh salad leaves.**

SERVES 6

*3 boneless Barbary duck breasts, about 250 g/8 oz each
salt • assorted salad leaves, to serve*

Dressing:

*125 ml/4 fl oz/½ cup olive oil • 2 tsp sesame oil
2 tbsp lime juice • grated rind and juice of 1 orange
2 tsp Thai fish sauce • 1 tbsp grated ginger root
1 garlic clove, crushed • 2 tsp light soy sauce
3 spring onions (scallions), finely chopped • 1 tsp sugar*

1 Wash the duck breasts, dry on paper towels, then cut in half. Prick the skin all over with a fork and season well with salt.

2 Place the duck pieces, skin-side down, on a wire rack or trivet over a roasting tin (pan). Cook the duck in a preheated oven at 200°C/400°F/Gas Mark 6 for 10 minutes.

3 Turn the duck pieces over and cook for 12–15 minutes, or until the duck is cooked, but still pink in the centre, and the skin is crisp.

4 To make the dressing, beat the oils with the lime juice, orange rind and juice, fish sauce, ginger, garlic, soy sauce, spring onions (scallions) and sugar until well blended.

5 Remove the duck from the oven, allow to cool, then cut into thick slices. Add a little dressing to moisten and coat the duck.

6 To serve, arrange the salad leaves on a serving dish. Top with the sliced duck breasts and drizzle with the remaining dressing. Serve at once.

Duck with Lime & Kiwi Fruit

Tender breast of duck served in thin slices with a sweet but very tangy sauce.

SERVES 4

4 boneless or part-boned duck breasts
2 large limes • 2 tbsp sunflower oil
4 spring onions (scallions), thinly sliced diagonally
125 g/ 4 oz carrots, cut into matchsticks
6 tbsp dry white wine • 60 g/ 2 oz/⅓ cup sugar
2 kiwi fruit, peeled, halved and sliced • salt and pepper
parsley sprigs and lime halves, to garnish

1 Remove any excess fat from the duck breasts, then prick the skin all over with a fork or skewer and lay in a shallow dish in a single layer.

2 Remove the rind from the limes using a zester or grater and put into a bowl. Squeeze the juice from the limes (there should be 3 tablespoons or more; if not make up with lemon juice) and add to the bowl. Pour half the lime marinade over the duck breasts. Leave to stand in a cool place for at least 1 hour, turning at least once.

3 Drain the duck breasts. Heat 1 tablespoon of oil in the wok, swirling it around until really hot. Add the duck and fry quickly to seal all over. Lower the heat and cook for 5 minutes, turning several times until just cooked through and well browned. Remove and keep warm.

4 Wipe the wok clean with paper towels and heat the remaining oil in it. Add the spring onions (scallions) and carrots and stir-fry for about 1 minute then add the remaining lime marinade, wine and sugar. Bring to the boil and simmer for 2–3 minutes until slightly syrupy.

5 Add the duck breasts to the sauce, season well and add the kiwi fruit. Cook for about 1 minute until really hot and both the duck and kiwi fruit are well coated in the sauce.

6 Cut each duck breast into 'hinged' slices, open out into a fan shape and arrange on serving plates. Spoon the sauce over the duck, sprinkle with the remaining lime peel and garnish with parsley sprigs and lime halves.

Aromatic & Crispy Duck

The pancakes traditionally served with this dish take ages to make. Buy ready-made ones, or use crisp lettuce instead.

SERVES 4

2 large duck quarters • 1 tsp salt
3–4 pieces star anise • 1 tsp Szechuan red peppercorns
1 tsp cloves • 2 cinnamon sticks, broken into pieces
2–3 spring onions (scallions), cut into short sections
4–5 small slices ginger root
3–4 tbsp rice wine or dry sherry
vegetable oil for deep-frying

To serve:

12 ready-made pancakes or 12 crisp lettuce leaves
hoi-sin or plum sauce • ¼ cucumber, shredded thinly
3–4 spring onions (scallions), shredded thinly

1 Rub the duck pieces with the salt and arrange the star anise, peppercorns, cloves and cinnamon on top. Sprinkle with the spring onions (scallions), ginger and wine and leave to marinate for at least 3–4 hours.

2 Arrange the duck pieces (with the marinade spices) on a plate that will fit inside a bamboo steamer. Pour some hot water into a wok, place the bamboo steamer in the wok, sitting on a trivet. Put in the duck and cover with the bamboo lid. Steam the duck pieces over a high heat for at least 2–3 hours, until tender and cooked through. Top up the hot water from time to time.

3 Remove the duck and leave to cool for at least 4–5 hours – this is very important, for unless the duck is cold and dry, it will not be very crispy.

4 Pour off the water and wipe the wok dry. Pour in the oil and heat until

smoking. Deep-fry the duck pieces, skin-side down, for 4–5 minutes or until crisp and brown. Remove and drain on paper towels.

5 To serve, scrape the meat off the bone, place about 1 teaspoon of hoi-sin or plum sauce on the centre of a pancake or lettuce leaf and add a few pieces of cucumber, spring onion (scallion) and duck meat. Wrap up to form a small parcel and eat with your fingers. Provide plenty of paper napkins for your guests.

Red Spiced Beef

A spicy stir-fry flavoured with paprika, chilli and tomato, with a crisp bite to it from the celery strips.

SERVES 4

*625 g / 1¼ lb sirloin or rump steak • 2 tbsp paprika
2–3 tsp mild chilli powder • ½ tsp salt • 6 celery stalks
6 tbsp stock or water • 2 tbsp tomato purée (paste)
2 tbsp clear honey • 3 tbsp wine vinegar
1 tbsp Worcestershire sauce • 2 tbsp sunflower oil
4 spring onions (scallions), thinly sliced diagonally
4 tomatoes, peeled, deseeded and sliced
1–2 garlic cloves, crushed • Chinese noodles, to serve
celery leaves, to garnish (optional)*

1 Cut the steak across the grain into narrow strips 1 cm/½ inch thick and place in a bowl. Combine the paprika, chilli powder and salt. Add to the beef and mix until the meat strips are evenly coated with the spices. Cover and leave to marinate for at least 30 minutes.

2 Cut the celery into 5 cm /2 inch lengths, then slice into strips about 5 mm/ ¼ inch thick.

3 Combine the stock, tomato purée (paste), honey, vinegar and Worcestershire sauce in a bowl.

4 Heat the oil in the wok, swirling it around until really hot. Add the spring onions (scallions), celery, tomatoes and garlic, and stir-fry for about 1 minute until the vegetables are beginning to soften. Then add the steak strips and stir-fry over a high heat for 3–4 minutes until the meat is well sealed.

5 Add the sauce to the wok and continue to stir-fry briskly until thoroughly coated and sizzling.

6 Serve with noodles and garnish with celery leaves, if using.

Sukiyaki Beef

An easy way of giving beef a Japanese flavour is to marinate it in teriyaki sauce and sherry for anything from 1 to 24 hours.

SERVES 4

2.5 cm/1 inch piece of ginger root, grated
1 garlic clove, crushed • 4 tbsp sherry • 4 tbsp teriyaki sauce
500–625 g/1 lb 2 oz–1¼ lb sirloin, rump or fillet steak
1 × 400 g/14 oz can of hearts of palm
2 tbsp sesame or sunflower oil
125 g/4 oz button or closed cup mushrooms, thinly sliced
salt and pepper

To garnish:
sesame seeds (optional) • spring onion (scallion) tassels

1 Blend the ginger in a shallow dish with the garlic, sherry and teriyaki sauce, adding a little salt.

2 Cut the steak across the grain into narrow strips about 2.5–4 cm/1–1½ inches long. Add to the marinade in the dish, mix thoroughly to coat, cover and leave in a cool place for 1–24 hours.

3 Drain the hearts of palm and cut into slanting slices about 1 cm/½ inch thick.

4 Remove the beef from the marinade with a slotted spoon, reserving the marinade. Heat the oil in the wok, swirling it around until really hot. Add the beef and stir-fry for 2 minutes, then add the mushrooms and continue to cook for 1 minute.

5 Add the hearts of palm to the wok with the reserved marinade and stir-fry for 1 minute, making sure the meat is evenly coated in the sauce. Adjust the seasoning, if necessary, and serve sprinkled with sesame seeds (if using) and garnished with spring onion (scallion) tassels.

Beef with Beans

Steak with a strong flavouring of sherry, teriyaki sauce and orange make an ideal dish for entertaining.

SERVES 4

500–625 g/ 1 lb 2 oz–1¼ lb sirloin, rump or fillet steak
1 orange • 2 tbsp sesame oil • 1 garlic clove, crushed
4 spring onions (scallions), thinly sliced diagonally
175 g/ 6 oz French (green) or fine beans, cut into 2–3 pieces
4 tbsp sherry • 1½ tbsp teriyaki sauce
1¼ tsp ground allspice • 1 tsp sugar
1 × 400 g/ 14 oz can of cannellini beans, drained
salt and pepper

To garnish:
orange slices • fresh bay leaves

1 Cut the steak into narrow strips, 4 cm/1½ inches long, cutting across the grain.

2 Remove the peel from the orange using a citrus zester, or pare thinly with a potato peeler, and cut the rind into julienne strips. Squeeze the orange and reserve the juice.

3 Heat 1 tablespoon of the oil in the wok, swirling it around until really hot. Add the strips of beef and stir-fry for 2 minutes, then remove from the wok and keep warm.

4 Add the remaining oil to the wok and when hot add the garlic and spring onions (scallions) and stir-fry for 1–2 minutes. Add the French (green) beans and cook for 2 minutes. Add the sherry, teriyaki sauce, orange rind and 3 tablespoons of orange juice, allspice, sugar and seasoning and when mixed return the beef and any juices to the wok. Stir-fry for 1–2 minutes then add the cannellini beans and stir until hot. Adjust the seasoning. Serve garnished with orange slices and bay leaves.

Beef & Chilli Black Bean Sauce

You don't need to use expensive cuts of beef steak for this recipe: the meat will be tender as it is cut into thin slices and marinated.

SERVES 4

250–300 g/ 8–10 oz beef steak (such as rump)
1 small onion
1 small green (bell) pepper, cored and deseeded
about 300 ml/ ½ pint/ 1¼ cups vegetable oil
1 spring onion (scallion), cut into short sections
a few small slices of ginger root
1–2 small green or red chillies, deseeded and sliced
2 tbsp crushed black bean sauce

Marinade:

½ tsp bicarbonate of soda (baking soda) or baking powder
½ tsp sugar • 1 tbsp light soy sauce
2 tsp rice wine or dry sherry
2 tsp Cornflour (Cornstarch) Paste (see page 22)
2 tsp sesame oil

1 Cut the beef into thin strips. Mix the marinade ingredients in a shallow dish, add the beef strips, turn to coat and leave to marinate for at least 2–3 hours – the longer the better.

2 Cut the onion and green (bell) pepper into small equal-sized squares.

3 Heat the oil in a preheated wok. Add the beef strips and stir-fry for 1 minute, or until the colour changes. Remove with a slotted spoon and drain on paper towels. Keep warm.

4 Pour off the excess oil, leaving about 1 tablespoon in the wok.

Add the spring onion (scallion), ginger, chillies, onion and green (bell) pepper and stir-fry for about 1 minute. Add the black bean sauce, stir until smooth then return the beef strips to the wok. Blend well and stir-fry for 1 minute. Serve hot with boiled rice.

Oyster Sauce Beef

As in Stir-Fried Pork with Vegetables (page 106), the vegetables can be varied as you wish.

SERVES 4

300 g / 10 oz beef steak
1 tsp sugar • 1 tbsp light soy sauce
1 tsp rice wine or dry sherry
1 tsp Cornflour (Cornstarch) Paste (see page 22)
½ small carrot
60 g / 2 oz mangetout (snow peas)
60 g / 2 oz canned bamboo shoots
60 g / 2 oz canned straw mushrooms
about 300 ml / ½ pint / 1¼ cups vegetable oil
1 spring onion (scallion), cut into short sections
2–3 small slices of ginger root • ½ tsp salt
2 tbsp oyster sauce
2–3 tbsp Chinese Stock (see page 24) or water

1 Cut the beef into small, thin slices. Place in a shallow dish with the sugar, soy sauce, wine and cornflour (cornstarch) paste, turn to coat and leave to marinate for 25–30 minutes.

2 Slice the carrots, mangetout (snow peas), bamboo shoots and straw mushrooms so that as far as possible the vegetable pieces are of uniform size and thickness.

3 Heat the oil in a preheated wok and add the beef slices. Stir-fry for 1 minute, then remove with a slotted spoon and keep warm.

4 Pour off the excess oil, leaving about 1 tablespoon in the wok. Add the sliced vegetables with the spring onion (scallion) and ginger, and stir-fry for about 2 minutes. Add the salt, beef, oyster sauce and stock or water. Blend well until heated through, and serve.

Ma-Po Tofu (Bean Curd)

**Ma-Po, the wife of a Szechuan chef,
created this dish in the 19th century.
Replace the beef with dried mushrooms to
make a vegetarian meal.**

SERVES 4

3 cakes tofu (bean curd)
3 tbsp vegetable oil
125 g/4 oz coarsely minced (ground) beef
½ tsp finely chopped garlic
1 leek, cut into short sections
½ tsp salt
1 tbsp black bean sauce
1 tbsp light soy sauce
1 tsp chilli bean sauce
3–4 tbsp Chinese Stock (see page 24) or water
2 tsp Cornflour (Cornstarch) Paste (see page 22)
a few drops of sesame oil
black pepper
finely chopped spring onions (scallions), to garnish

1 Cut the tofu (bean curd) into 1 cm/½ inch cubes, handling it carefully. Bring some water to the boil in a pan or a wok, add the tofu (bean curd) and blanch for 2–3 minutes to harden. Remove and drain well.

2 Heat the oil in a preheated wok. Add the minced (ground) beef and garlic, and stir-fry for 1 minute, or until the beef changes colour. Add the leek, salt and sauces, and blend well. Add the stock or water and the tofu (bean curd). Bring to the boil and braise for 2–3 minutes.

3 Add the cornflour (cornstarch) paste, and stir until the sauce has thickened. Sprinkle with sesame oil and black pepper, and garnish with spring onions (scallions).

Peppered Beef Cashew

A simple but stunning dish of tender strips of beef mixed with vegetables and crunchy cashew nuts, coated in a hot sauce. Serve with rice noodles.

SERVES 4

1 tbsp groundnut or sunflower oil
1 tbsp sesame oil
1 onion, sliced
1 garlic clove, crushed
1 tbsp grated ginger root
500 g/ 1 lb 2 oz fillet or rump steak, cut into thin strips
2 tsp palm sugar or demerara sugar
2 tbsp light soy sauce
1 small yellow (bell) pepper, cored, deseeded and sliced
1 red (bell) pepper, cored, deseeded and sliced
4 spring onions (scallions), chopped
2 celery stalks, chopped
4 large open-cap mushrooms, sliced
4 tbsp roasted cashew nuts
3 tbsp stock or white wine
rice noodles, to serve

1 Heat the oils in a wok or large, heavy-based frying pan (skillet). Add the onion, garlic and ginger, and stir-fry for about 2 minutes until softened and lightly coloured.

2 Add the steak strips and stir-fry for 2–3 minutes, until the meat has browned. Add the sugar and soy sauce, mixing well.

3 Add the (bell) peppers, spring onions (scallions), celery, mushrooms and cashews, mixing well.

4 Add the stock or wine and stir-fry for 2–3 minutes until the beef is cooked through and the vegetables are tender-crisp. Serve immediately with rice noodles.

Beef & Bok Choy

**A colourful selection of vegetables stir-fried
with tender strips of steak.**

SERVES 4

*1 large head of bok choy, about 250–275 g/ 8–9 oz, torn
into large pieces
2 tbsp vegetable oil
2 garlic cloves, crushed
500 g/ 1 lb 2 oz rump or fillet steak,
cut into thin strips
150 g/ 5 oz mangetout (snow peas), trimmed
150 g/ 5 oz baby sweetcorn cobs
6 spring onions (scallions), chopped
2 red (bell) peppers, cored, deseeded and thinly sliced
2 tbsp oyster sauce
1 tbsp fish sauce
1 tbsp sugar
rice or noodles, to serve*

1 Steam the bok choy leaves over boiling water until just tender. Keep warm.

2 Heat the oil in a large, heavy-based frying pan (skillet) or wok, add the garlic and steak strips and stir-fry until just browned, about 1–2 minutes.

3 Add the mangetout (snow peas), baby sweetcorn cobs, spring onions (scallions), (bell) pepper, oyster sauce, fish sauce and sugar, mixing well. Stir-fry for 2–3 minutes until the vegetables are just tender, but still quite crisp to the bite.

4 Arrange the bok choy leaves in the base of a warmed serving dish and spoon the beef and vegetable mixture into the centre.

5 Serve the stir-fry immediately, with rice or noodles.

Green Beef Curry

This is a quickly-made curry of beef steak strips, cubed aubergine (eggplant) and onion in a cream sauce flavoured wth green curry paste. Serve with fluffy rice and a salad.

SERVES 4

1 aubergine (eggplant), peeled and cubed
2 onions, cut into thin wedges • 2 tbsp vegetable oil
Green Curry Paste (see page 66)
500 g/ 1 lb 2 oz beef fillet, cut into thin strips
500 ml/ 16 fl oz/ 2 cups thick coconut milk or cream
2 tbsp fish sauce • 1 tbsp brown sugar
1 red chilli, deseeded and very finely chopped
1 green chilli, deseeded and very finely chopped
2.5 cm/ 1 inch piece of ginger root, finely chopped
4 kaffir lime leaves, torn into pieces
chopped fresh basil and lime wedges, to garnish
rice and green salad leaves, to serve

1 Blanch the aubergine (eggplant) cubes and onion wedges in boiling water for about 2 minutes, to soften. Drain thoroughly.

2 Heat the oil in a large heavy-based pan or wok, add the curry paste and cook for 1 minute.

3 Add the beef strips and stir-fry, over a high heat, for about 1 minute, to brown on all sides.

4 Add the coconut milk or cream, fish sauce and sugar to the pan and bring the mixture to the boil, stirring constantly.

5 Add the aubergine (eggplant) and onion, chillies, ginger and lime leaves. Cook for 2 minutes.

6 Transfer the curry to a warmed serving dish. Garnish with the basil leaves and lime wedges, and serve with rice and a green salad.

Five-Spice Lamb

Five-spice powder is a blend of ginger, cinnamon, fennel, star anise and cloves.

SERVES 4

625 g/ 1½ lb lean boneless lamb (leg or fillet)
2 tsp Chinese five-spice powder • 3 tbsp sunflower oil
1 red (bell) pepper, cored, deseeded and sliced thinly
1 green (bell) pepper, cored, deseeded and sliced thinly
1 yellow or orange (bell) pepper, cored, deseeded and sliced thinly
4–6 spring onions (scallions), sliced thinly diagonally
175 g/ 6 oz French (green) or fine beans,
cut into 4 cm/ 1½ inch lengths
2 tbsp soy sauce • 4 tbsp sherry
salt and pepper • Chinese noodles, to serve

To garnish:
strips of red and yellow (bell) pepper
fresh coriander (cilantro) leaves

1 Cut the lamb into narrow strips, about 4 cm/1½ inches long, across the grain. Place in a bowl, add the five-spice powder and ¼ teaspoon of salt, mix well and leave to marinate, covered, in a cool place for at least 1 hour and up to 24 hours.

2 Heat half the oil in the wok, swirling it around until really hot. Add the lamb and stir-fry briskly for 3–4 minutes until almost cooked. Remove from the wok.

3 Add the remaining oil to the wok and when hot add the (bell) peppers and spring onions (scallions). Stir-fry for 2–3 minutes, then add the beans and stir for 1 minute. Add the soy sauce and sherry and when hot add the lamb and any juices. Stir-fry for 1–2 minutes until the lamb is hot and coated in the sauce. Season and serve with noodles, garnished with strips of (bell) pepper and fresh coriander (cilantro).

Lamb Biryani

In India this elaborate, beautifully coloured dish is usually served on festive occasions.

SERVES 4

250 g / 8 oz / 1¼ cups basmati rice, rinsed and soaked in cold water for 30 minutes
2 garlic cloves, peeled and left whole
2.5 cm / 1 inch piece of ginger root, grated • 4 cloves
2 green cardamom pods • ½ tsp black peppercorns
1 tsp cumin seeds • 1 tsp coriander seeds
2.5 cm / 1 inch piece cinnamon stick
1 tsp saffron strands • 50 ml / 2 fl oz / 4 tbsp tepid water
2 tbsp ghee • 2 shallots, sliced
¼ tsp grated nutmeg • ¼ tsp chilli powder
500 g / 1 lb 2 oz boneless lamb, cut into 2.5 cm / 1 inch cubes
180 ml / 6 fl oz / ¾ cup natural yogurt
30 g / 1 oz / 2 tbsp sultanas (golden raisins)
30 g / 1 oz / ¼ cup flaked (slivered) almonds, toasted

1 Bring a large saucepan of salted water to the boil. Add the rice and boil for 6 minutes. Drain and set aside.

2 Grind together the garlic, ginger, cloves, cardamom pods, peppercorns, cumin, coriander and cinnamon.

3 Combine the saffron and water, and set aside. Heat the ghee in a large saucepan and add the shallots. Fry until golden brown then add the ground spice mix, nutmeg and chilli powder. Stir for 1 minute and add the lamb. Cook until evenly browned. Add the yogurt, stirring constantly, then the sultanas (golden raisins) and bring to a simmer. Cook for 40 minutes, stirring occasionally.

4 Carefully pile the rice on to the sauce, in a pyramid shape. Trickle the saffron solution over the rice in lines. Cover the pan with a clean tea towel and put on the lid. Reduce the heat to low and

cook for 10 minutes. Remove the lid and tea towel, and quickly make 3 holes in the rice with a wooden spoon handle, to the level of the sauce, but not touching it. Replace the tea towel and the lid and leave to stand for 5 minutes.

5 Remove the lid and tea towel, lightly fork the rice and serve, sprinkled with the toasted almonds.

Lamb Do Pyaza

Do Pyaza usually indicates a dish of meat cooked with onions, and in this recipe the onions are cooked in two different ways.

SERVES 4

2 tbsp ghee • 2 large onions, sliced finely
4 garlic cloves, 2 of them crushed
750 g/ 1½ lb boneless lamb, cut into 2.5 cm/ 1 inch cubes
1 tsp chilli powder
2.5 cm/ 1 inch piece of ginger root, grated
2 fresh green chillies, chopped • ½ tsp ground turmeric
180 ml/ 6 fl oz/ ¾ cup natural yogurt • 2 cloves
2.5 cm/ 1 inch piece cinnamon stick
300 ml/ ½ pint/ 1¼ cups water
2 tbsp chopped fresh coriander (cilantro)
3 tbsp lemon juice • salt and pepper
naan bread, to serve

1 Heat the ghee in a large pan and add 1 of the onions and all the garlic. Cook for 2–3 minutes, stirring constantly. Add the lamb and brown all over. Remove the lamb and set aside.

2 Add the chilli powder, ginger, chillies and turmeric and stir for a further 30 seconds. Season to taste, then add the yogurt, cloves, cinnamon and water. Return the lamb to the pan. Bring to the boil then simmer for 10 minutes.

3 Transfer the mixture to an ovenproof dish and cook uncovered in a preheated oven, 180°C/ 350°F/Gas Mark 4, for 40 minutes. Adjust the seasoning, if necessary.

4 Stir in the remaining onion and cook for a further 40 minutes. Add the fresh coriander (cilantro) and lemon juice, and stir. Serve hot, accompanied by naan bread.

Vindaloo Curry

Vindaloo is the classic fiery curry from Goa.

SERVES 4

100 ml/ 3½ fl oz/ scant ½ cup oil
1 large onion, sliced into half rings
120 ml/ 4 fl oz/ ½ cup white wine vinegar
300 ml/ ½ pint/ 1¼ cups water
750 g/ 1½ lb boneless pork, diced • 2 tsp cumin seeds
4 dried red chillies • 1 tsp black peppercorns
6 green cardamom pods
2.5 cm/ 1 inch piece cinnamon stick
1 tsp black mustard seeds • 3 cloves
1 tsp fenugreek seeds • 2 tbsp ghee
4 garlic cloves, chopped finely
3.5 cm/ 1½ inch piece of ginger root, chopped finely
1 tbsp coriander seeds, ground
2 tomatoes, skinned and chopped
250 g/ 8 oz potato, cut into 1 cm/ ½ inch cubes
1 tsp light brown sugar • ½ tsp ground turmeric
salt • basmati rice and pickles, to serve

1 Heat the oil in a large saucepan and fry the onion until golden brown. Set aside.

2 Combine 2 tablespoons of the vinegar with 1 tablespoon of the water in a large bowl. Add the pork and mix well. Set aside.

3 In a blender mix the onion, cumin, chillies, peppercorns, cardamom, cinnamon, mustard seeds, cloves and fenugreek to a paste. Alternatively, grind the ingredients together with a pestle and mortar. Transfer to a bowl and add the remaining vinegar.

4 Heat the ghee in a frying pan (skillet) or casserole, add the pork and cook until it is browned on all sides. Add the garlic, ginger and ground coriander and stir

until fragrant. Add the tomatoes, potato, brown sugar, turmeric and remaining water. Add salt to taste and bring to the boil.

Stir in the spice paste, cover and reduce the heat, and simmer for 1 hour. Serve with basmati rice and pickles.

Deep-Fried Spare Ribs

**The spare ribs should be chopped
into small bite-sized pieces before or
after cooking.**

SERVES 4

*8–10 finger spare ribs
1 tsp five-spice powder or 1 tbsp mild curry powder
1 tbsp rice wine or dry sherry
1 egg • 2 tbsp flour
vegetable oil, for deep-frying
1 tsp finely shredded spring onions (scallions)
1 tsp finely shredded fresh green or red hot chillies, deseeded
salt and pepper*

Spicy salt & pepper:
*1 tbsp salt • 1 tsp five-spice powder
1 tsp ground Szechuan peppercorns*

1 Chop the ribs into 3–4 small pieces. Place the ribs in a bowl with salt and pepper to taste, five-spice or curry powder and the wine or sherry. Turn to coat the ribs in the spices and leave them to marinate for 1–2 hours.

2 Make the Spicy Salt & Pepper by combining the ground spices in a small bowl.

3 Mix the egg and flour together to make a batter. Dip the ribs in the batter one by one. Heat the oil in a preheated wok until smoking. Deep-fry the ribs for 4–5 minutes, then remove with a slotted spoon, and drain on paper towels. Return the ribs to the hot oil and fry again for 1 minute. Remove and drain on paper towels again.

4 Pour 1 tablespoon of the hot oil over the spring onions (scallions) and chillies and leave for 30–40 seconds. Serve the ribs with Spicy Salt & Pepper, garnished with the shredded spring onions (scallions) and chillies.

Pork Balls with Minted Sauce

Made with lean minced pork, the balls are braised with stock and pickled walnuts to give a tangy flavour.

SERVES 4

500 g/ 1 lb 2 oz lean minced pork
45 g/ 1½ oz/³⁄₄ cup fine fresh white breadcrumbs
½ tsp ground allspice • 1 garlic clove, crushed
2 tbsp freshly chopped mint
1 egg, beaten • 2 tbsp sunflower oil
1 red (bell) pepper, cored, deseeded and thinly sliced
250 ml/ 8 fl oz/ 1 cup chicken stock
4 pickled walnuts, sliced • salt and pepper
rice or Chinese noodles, to serve
fresh mint, to garnish

1 Combine the pork, breadcrumbs, seasoning, allspice, garlic and half the chopped mint in a bowl, then bind together with the egg. Dampen your hands and shape the meat mixture into 20 small balls.

2 Heat the oil in the wok, swirling it around until really hot, then stir-fry the pork balls until browned all over, about 4–5 minutes. Remove from the wok with a slotted spoon and drain thoroughly on paper towels.

3 Pour off all but 1 tablespoon of the fat and oil from the wok then add the red (bell) pepper and stir-fry for 2–3 minutes, or until softened, but not coloured. Add the stock and bring to the boil. Season well and add the pork balls, stirring to coat in the sauce; simmer for 7–10 minutes, turning occasionally. Add the remaining chopped mint and the pickled walnuts and continue to simmer for 2–3 minutes, turning the pork balls regularly to coat in the sauce.

4 Adjust the seasoning and serve with rice or Chinese noodles, or with a stir-fried vegetable dish, garnished with sprigs of fresh mint.

Stir-Fried Pork with Vegetables

This is a basic 'meat and veg' recipe – using pork, chicken, beef or lamb, and vegetables according to seasonal availability.

SERVES 4

250 g / 8 oz pork fillet • 1 tsp sugar
1 tbsp light soy sauce • 1 tsp rice wine or dry sherry
1 tsp Cornflour (Cornstarch) Paste (see page 22)
1 small carrot
1 small green (bell) pepper, cored and deseeded
about 175 g / 6 oz Chinese leaves • 4 tbsp vegetable oil
1 spring onion (scallion), cut into short sections
a few small slices of peeled ginger root • 1 tsp salt
2–3 tbsp Chinese Stock (see page 24) or water
a few drops of sesame oil

1 Slice the pork fillet into small pieces and place in a shallow dish. Add half the sugar, half the soy sauce, the wine and cornflour (cornstarch) paste, turn to coat and leave in the refrigerator to marinate for 10–15 minutes.

2 Cut the carrot, green (bell) pepper and Chinese leaves into slices the same size as the pork pieces.

3 Heat the oil in a preheated wok and stir-fry the pork for about 1 minute to seal in the flavour. Remove with a slotted spoon and keep warm.

4 Add the carrot, (bell) pepper, Chinese leaves, spring onion (scallion) and ginger to the wok and stir-fry for 2 minutes. Add the salt and remaining sugar, followed by the pork and remaining soy sauce, and the stock or water. Blend and stir-fry for 1–2 minutes until hot. Sprinkle with the sesame oil and serve.

Fish & Seafood

China's coastline, rivers and lakes offer a wide variety of fresh and salt-water fish and seafood. The coastline of India, too, means that fish and seafood are popular in some areas, where it plays an important part in the diet. Whatever the fish, the golden rule is to choose seafood that is at the absolute peak of freshness!

Sole Paupiette

A delicate dish of sole fillets rolled up with spinach and prawns (shrimp), and served in a creamy ginger sauce.

SERVES 4

125 g/ 4 oz fresh young spinach leaves
2 Dover soles or large lemon soles or plaice, filleted
125 g/ 4 oz peeled prawns (shrimp), defrosted if frozen
2 tsp sunflower oil
2–4 spring onions (scallions), finely sliced diagonally
2 thin slices of ginger root, finely chopped
150 ml/ ¼ pint/ ⅔ cup fish stock or water
2 tsp cornflour (cornstarch) • 4 tbsp single (light) cream
6 tbsp natural yogurt • salt and pepper
whole prawns (shrimp), to garnish (optional)

1 Strip the stalks off the spinach, rinse and dry on paper towels. Divide the spinach between the seasoned fish fillets, laying the leaves on the skin side. Divide half the prawns (shrimp) between them. Roll up the fillets from head to tail and secure with wooden cocktail sticks (toothpicks). Arrange on a plate in a bamboo steamer.

2 Stand a low metal trivet in the wok, add enough water to almost reach the top of it and bring to the boil. Place the bamboo steamer on the trivet, cover with the steamer lid and then the wok lid, or cover tightly with a domed piece of foil. Steam gently for 30 minutes until the fish is tender and cooked through. Remove the fish rolls and keep warm. Empty the wok and wipe dry.

3 Heat the oil in the wok, swirling it around until really hot. Add the spring onions (scallions) and ginger and stir-fry for 1–2 minutes. Add the stock and bring to the boil.

4 Blend the cornflour (cornstarch) with the

cream in a small bowl. Add the yogurt and remaining prawns (shrimp) to the wok and heat gently until boiling. Add a little sauce to the blended cream and add to the wok. Heat gently until thickened. Adjust the seasoning. Spoon the sauce over the paupiettes and garnish with whole prawns (shrimp), if liked.

Bajan Fish

Bajan seasoning comes from Barbados and can be used with all meat, fish, poultry and game. Add more chilli to make it really hot.

SERVES 4

500-625 g/ 1 lb 2 oz–1¼ lb monkfish tails, boned and cubed
2 large carrots • 175–250 g/ 6–8 oz baby sweetcorn cobs
3 tbsp sunflower oil
1 yellow (bell) pepper, cored, deseeded and thinly sliced
1 tbsp wine vinegar
150 ml/¼ pint/²⁄₃ cup fish or vegetable stock
1 tbsp lemon juice • 2 tbsp sherry
1 tsp cornflour (cornstarch) • salt and pepper
fresh herbs and lemon slices, to garnish

Bajan seasoning:
1 small onion, quartered • 2 shallots
3–4 garlic cloves, crushed
4–6 large spring onions (scallions), sliced
small handful of fresh parsley • 2–3 sprigs of fresh thyme
small strip of green chilli pepper, deseeded,
or ½–¼ tsp chilli powder
½ tsp salt • ¼ tsp freshly ground black pepper
2 tbsp brown rum or red wine vinegar

1 First make the Bajan seasoning. Place all the ingredients in a food processor and process very finely.

(plastic wrap) and leave to marinate in the refrigerator for at least 30 minutes, preferably overnight.

2 Spread the Bajan seasoning in a shallow dish and press the fish into the seasoning, turning to coat evenly. Cover with cling film

3 Cut the carrots into narrow 4 cm/1½ inch slices and slice the baby sweetcorn cobs diagonally.

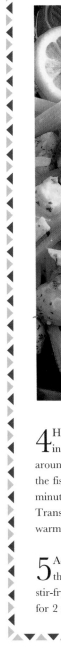

4 Heat 2 tablespoons of oil in the wok, swirling it around until really hot. Add the fish and stir-fry for 3–4 minutes until cooked through. Transfer to a bowl and keep warm.

5 Add the remaining oil to the wok and when hot stir-fry the carrots and corn for 2 minutes, then add the (bell) pepper and stir-fry for 1–2 minutes. Return the fish and juices to the wok and stir-fry for 1–2 minutes.

6 Blend the vinegar, stock, lemon juice, sherry and seasoning with the cornflour (cornstarch). Stir into the wok and boil until the sauce thickens. Serve garnished with herbs and lemon slices.

Fish with Saffron Sauce

White steamed fish is served with a light creamy saffron sauce with a real bite to it.

SERVES 4

625–750 g/ 1¼ – 1½ lb white fish fillets
(cod, haddock, whiting etc.)
pinch of Chinese five-spice powder • 4 sprigs of fresh thyme
large pinch of saffron threads
250 ml/ 8 fl oz/ 1 cup boiling fish or vegetable stock
2 tbsp sunflower oil
125 g/ 4 oz button mushrooms, thinly sliced
grated rind of ½ lemon • 1 tbsp lemon juice
½ tsp freshly chopped thyme or ¼ tsp dried thyme
½ bunch watercress, chopped • 1½ tsp cornflour (cornstarch)
3 tbsp single (light) or double (heavy) cream • salt and pepper
lemon wedges and watercress sprigs, to garnish

1 Skin the fish and cut into 4 even-sized portions. Season with salt and pepper and five-spice powder. Arrange the fish on a plate and place in the bottom of a bamboo steamer, laying a sprig of thyme on each piece of fish (if the fillets are large you may need 2 steamers, one on top of the other).

2 Stand a low metal trivet in a wok and add water to almost reach the top of it. Bring to the boil, stand the bamboo steamer on the trivet and cover with the bamboo lid and then the wok lid, or a domed piece of foil. Simmer for 20 minutes or until the fish is tender, adding more boiling water to the wok as necessary.

3 Meanwhile, soak the saffron threads in the boiling stock.

4 When the fish is tender, remove and keep warm. Empty the wok and wipe dry. Heat the oil in the wok, add the mushrooms and stir-fry for about 2 minutes. Add the saffron stock, lemon rind and

juice and chopped thyme and bring to the boil. Add the watercress and simmer for a 1–2 minutes.

5 Blend the cornflour (cornstarch) with the cream, add a little of the sauce from the wok, mix well, return to the wok and heat gently until thickened. Pour the sauce over the fish and serve, garnished with lemon wedges and watercress.

Sesame Salmon & Cream Sauce

Salmon fillets hold their shape when tossed in sesame seeds and stir-fried.

SERVES 4

625–750 g / 1¼–1½ lb salmon or pink trout fillets
2 tbsp light soy sauce • 3 tbsp sesame seeds
3 tbsp sunflower oil
4 spring onions (scallions), thinly sliced diagonally
2 large courgettes (zucchini), diced,
or 12 cm / 5 inch piece of cucumber, diced
grated rind of ½ lemon • 1 tbsp lemon juice
½ tsp turmeric • 6 tbsp fish stock or water
3 tbsp double (heavy) cream or fromage frais
salt and pepper • frisee (chicory), to garnish (optional)

1 Skin the salmon and cut into strips approximately 4 × 2.5 cm / 1½ × 1 inches. Pat dry on paper towels. Season lightly, then brush with soy sauce and sprinkle all over with sesame seeds.

2 Heat 2 tablespoons of oil in the wok, swirling it around until really hot.

3 Add the salmon and stir-fry for 3–4 minutes until lightly browned all over. Remove with a fish slice, drain on paper towels and keep warm.

4 Add the remaining oil to the wok and when hot add the spring onions (scallions) and courgettes (zucchini) or cucumber and stir-fry for 1–2 minutes. Add the lemon rind and juice, turmeric, stock and seasoning and bring the mixture to the boil for 1 minute. Stir the cream or fromage frais into the sauce.

5 Return the salmon to the wok and toss gently in the sauce until really hot. Serve on warm plates and garnish with frisee (chicory), if using.

Fish with Ginger Butter

Whole mackerel or trout are stuffed with herbs, wrapped in foil or banana leaves, baked and drizzled with a ginger butter.

SERVES 4

4 × 250 g/8 oz whole trout or mackerel, gutted
4 tbsp chopped fresh coriander (cilantro)
5 garlic cloves, crushed
2 tsp grated lemon or lime zest
2 tsp vegetable oil
banana leaves, for wrapping (optional)
90 g/3 oz/6 tbsp butter
1 tbsp grated ginger root
1 tbsp light soy sauce • salt and pepper

To garnish:
sprigs of fresh coriander (cilantro)
lemon or lime wedges

1 Wash and dry the fish. Mix the coriander (cilantro) with the garlic, lemon or lime zest and salt and pepper to taste. Spoon into the fish cavities. Brush each fish with a little oil and season well with salt and pepper.

2 Place each fish on a double thickness of baking parchment or foil and wrap up well to enclose. Alternatively, wrap in banana leaves. Place on a baking sheet and bake in a preheated oven at 190°C/375°F/Gas Mark 5 for about 25 minutes or until the flesh will flake easily.

3 Meanwhile, melt the butter in a small pan. Add the grated ginger and stir until well mixed, then stir in the soy sauce.

4 To serve, unwrap the fish parcels, drizzle over the ginger butter and garnish with coriander (cilantro) and lemon or lime wedges.

Red Curry Fish Cakes

Thai fishcakes make a tasty starter and good introduction to a Thai-style meal.

SERVES 4–6

1 kg/ 2 lb fish fillets or prepared seafood, such as cod, haddock, prawns (shrimp), crab meat or lobster
1 egg, beaten • 2 tbsp chopped fresh coriander
Red Curry Paste (see page 64)
1 bunch spring onions (scallions), finely chopped
vegetable oil, for deep-frying • chilli flowers

Cucumber salad:
1 large cucumber, peeled and grated
2 shallots, peeled and grated
2 red chillies, deseeded and very finely chopped
2 tbsp fish sauce • 2 tbsp dried powdered shrimps
1½–2 tbsp lime juice

1 Place the fish in a blender or food processor with the egg, coriander and curry paste and purée until smooth and well blended. Turn the mixture into a bowl, add the spring onions (scallions) and mix well to combine.

2 Taking 2 tablespoons of the fish mixture at a time, shape into balls, then flatten them slightly with your fingers to make fishcakes.

3 Heat the oil in a wok or pan until hot, add a few of the fishcakes and deep-fry for 2–3 minutes until brown and cooked through. Remove with a slotted spoon and drain on paper towels. Keep warm while cooking the remaining fishcakes.

4 Meanwhile, to make the cucumber salad, mix the cucumber with the shallots, chillies, fish sauce, dried shrimps and lime juice.

5 Serve the warm fishcakes with cucumber salad.

Braised Fish Fillets

**Any white fish such as lemon sole or plaice
is ideal for this dish.**

SERVES 4

*3–4 small Chinese dried mushrooms
300–350 g/ 10–12 oz fish fillets • 1 tsp salt
½ egg white, lightly beaten
1 tsp Cornflour (Cornstarch) Paste (see page 22)
600 ml/ 1 pint/ 2½ cups vegetable oil
1 tsp finely chopped ginger root
2 spring onions (scallions), finely chopped
1 garlic clove, finely chopped
½ small green (bell) pepper, deseeded and cut into small cubes
½ small carrot, thinly sliced
60 g/ 2 oz canned sliced bamboo shoots, rinsed and drained
½ tsp sugar • 1 tbsp light soy sauce
1 tsp rice wine or dry sherry • 1 tbsp chilli bean sauce
2–3 tbsp Chinese Stock (see page 24) or water
a few drops of sesame oil*

1 Soak the dried mushrooms in warm water for 30 minutes, then drain on paper towels, reserving the soaking water for stock or soup. Squeeze the mushrooms to extract all the moisture, cut off and discard any hard stems and slice thinly.

2 Cut the fish into bite-sized pieces, then place in a dish and mix with a pinch of salt, the egg white and cornflour (cornstarch) paste, turning the fish to coat. Heat the oil to 180–190°C/ 350–375°F or until a cube of bread browns in 30 seconds and deep-fry the fish for 1 minute. Remove with a slotted spoon and drain.

3 Pour off the oil, leaving 1 tablespoon in the wok. Add the ginger, spring onions (scallions) and garlic to flavour the oil for a few seconds, then add the vegetables and stir-fry for 1 minute.

4 Add the sugar, soy sauce, wine, chilli bean sauce, stock or water, and remaining salt, and bring to the boil. Add the fish pieces, stir to coat well with the sauce, and braise for 1 minute. Sprinkle with sesame oil and serve immediately.

Green Fish Curry

This dish is from southern India. It has a wonderful fresh, hot, exotic taste resulting from the generous amount of fresh herbs, sharp fresh chillies and coconut milk.

SERVES 4

1 tbsp oil
2 spring onions (scallions), sliced
1 tsp cumin seeds, ground
2 fresh green chillies, chopped
1 tsp coriander seeds, ground
4 tbsp chopped fresh coriander (cilantro)
4 tbsp chopped fresh mint
1 tbsp chopped chives
150 ml/¼ pint/⅔ cup coconut milk
4 white fish fillets, about 250 g/8 oz each
salt and pepper
basmati rice, to serve
1 sprig of mint, to garnish

1 Heat the oil in a large frying pan (skillet) or shallow saucepan and add the spring onions (scallions). Stir-fry over a medium heat until they are softened but not coloured.

2 Stir in the cumin, chillies and ground coriander, and cook until aromatic. Add the fresh coriander (cilantro), mint, chives and coconut milk and season with salt and pepper to taste.

3 Carefully place the fish in the pan and poach for 10–15 minutes until the flesh flakes when tested with a fork.

4 Serve the fish curry with basmati rice and garnish with a mint sprig.

Masala Fried Fish

Frying fish is classically Indian, although it does not always spring to mind when thinking of Indian food.

SERVES 4–8

*8 plaice or other white fish fillets, about
125–150 g / 4–5 oz each
1 tbsp ground turmeric • 2 tbsp plain (all-purpose) flour
salt • ½ tsp black peppercorns, ground
1 tsp chilli powder • 1 tbsp coriander seeds, ground
1 garlic clove, crushed • 2 tsp Garam Masala (see page 9)
oil for deep frying*

To garnish:
chilli powder • lemon wedges

1 To skin the fish fillets, lay the fillet skin side down with the tail nearest you. Hold the tail end between your thumb and forefinger. Hold a sharp knife at a shallow angle to the fish in your other hand. Make an angled cut between the flesh and skin, then continue to cut the flesh from the skin until it is free.

2 In a shallow dish, combine the turmeric, flour, salt to taste, peppercorns, chilli powder, coriander seeds, garlic and garam masala. Mix well.

3 Fill a saucepan or a frying pan (skillet) with oil to a depth of 5–7 cm/2–3 inches, and heat to 180°C/350°F.

4 Coat the fish fillets in the spice mix either by shaking gently in a paper bag or turning over in the dish until well coated. Deep fry the fish fillets for about 3–5 minutes, turning often until the fish flakes easily with a fork. Drain on paper towels.

5 Serve sprinkled with chilli powder, garnished with lemon wedges.

Prawn (Shrimp) Bhuna

This is a fiery recipe with subtle undertones. As the flavour of the prawns (shrimp) should be noticeable, the spices should not take over this dish.

SERVES 4–6

2 dried red chillies, deseeded if liked
3 fresh green chillies, finely chopped
1 tsp ground turmeric
2 tsp white wine vinegar
½ tsp salt
3 garlic cloves, crushed
½ tsp pepper • 1 tsp paprika
500 g/1 lb 2 oz uncooked peeled king prawns (shrimp)
4 tbsp oil
1 onion, chopped very finely
180 ml/6 fl oz/³⁄₄ cup water
2 tbsp lemon juice
2 tsp Garam Masala (see page 9)
sprigs of fresh coriander (cilantro), to garnish

1 Combine the chillies, turmeric, vinegar, salt, garlic, pepper and paprika in a non-metallic bowl. Stir in the prawns (shrimp) and leave to marinate for 10 minutes.

2 Heat the oil in a large frying pan (skillet) or wok, add the onion and fry for 3–4 minutes until soft.

3 Add the prawns (shrimp) and spice mixture to the pan and stir-fry over a high heat for 2 minutes.

4 Reduce the heat, add the water and boil for 10 minutes, stirring occasionally, until the water has evaporated and the curry is fragrant. Stir in the lemon juice and garam masala.

5 Garnish with sprigs of fresh coriander (cilantro) and serve with rice.

Curried Crab

Shellfish is a major part of the diet in coastal areas of India. It is frozen and shipped to all parts India, to be used in a wide variety of dishes.

SERVES 4

2 tbsp mustard oil • 1 tbsp ghee
1 onion, chopped finely
5 cm/2 inch piece of ginger root, grated
2 garlic cloves, peeled but left whole
1 tsp ground turmeric • 1 tsp salt
1 tsp chilli powder
2 fresh green chillies, chopped
1 tsp paprika
125 g/4 oz/½ cup brown crab meat
350 g/12 oz/1½ cups white crab meat
250 ml/8 fl oz/1 cup natural yogurt
1 tsp Garam Masala (see page 9) • basmati rice, to serve
fresh coriander (cilantro), to garnish

1 Heat the mustard oil in a large, preferably non-stick, frying pan (skillet), wok or saucepan. When it starts to smoke add the ghee and onion. Stir for 3 minutes over a medium heat until the onion has softened.

2 Stir in the ginger and whole garlic cloves. Add the turmeric, salt, chilli powder, chillies and paprika. Mix thoroughly.

3 Increase the heat and add the crab meat and yogurt. Simmer, stirring occasionally, for 10 minutes until the sauce has thickened slightly. Add garam masala to taste.

4 Serve hot, over plain basmati rice, and garnished with fresh coriander (cilantro).

King Prawns (Jumbo Shrimp) in Red Curry Sauce

This inspired dish of prawns (shrimp) in a wonderfully spicy sauce is quick and simple, and will set your tasebuds alight!

SERVES 4

1 tbsp vegetable oil
6 spring onions (scallions), trimmed and sliced
1 stalk lemon grass
1 cm/½ inch piece of fresh ginger root
250 ml/8 fl oz/1 cup coconut milk
2 tbsp Red Curry Paste (page 64)
1 tbsp fish sauce
500 g/1 lb 2 oz uncooked king prawns (jumbo shrimp)
1 tbsp chopped fresh coriander (cilantro)
fresh chillies, to garnish

1 Heat the vegetable oil in a wok or large frying pan (skillet) and fry the spring onions (scallions) gently until softened, about 2 minutes.

2 Bruise the stalk of lemon grass using a meat mallet or rolling pin. Peel and finely grate the piece of fresh ginger root. Add the bruised lemon grass and grated ginger root to the wok or frying pan (skillet) with the coconut milk, red curry paste and fish sauce. Heat until almost boiling.

3 Peel the prawns (shrimp), leaving the tails intact. Remove the black vein running down the back of each prawn (shrimp). Add the prawns (shrimp) to the wok or frying pan (skillet) with the chopped coriander (cilantro) and cook gently for 5 minutes. Serve the prawns (shrimp) with the red curry sauce, garnished with fresh chillies.

Kaffir Lime Mussels with Lemon Grass

Fresh mussels with a Far Eastern flavour.

SERVES 4

750 g/ 1½ lb live mussels • 1 tbsp sesame oil
3 shallots, chopped finely • 2 garlic cloves, chopped finely
1 stalk lemon grass • 2 kaffir lime leaves
2 tbsp chopped fresh coriander (cilantro)
finely grated rind of 1 lime • 2 tbsp lime juice
300 ml/ ½ pint/ 1¼ cups hot vegetable stock
crusty bread to serve

To garnish:
sprigs of fresh coriander (cilantro) • lime wedges

1 Scrub the mussels well under cold running water, removing the 'beards'. Keep rinsing until there is no trace of sand. Discard any that are damaged or remain open when tapped.

2 Heat the sesame oil in a large saucepan and fry the shallots and garlic gently until softened, about 2 minutes. Bruise the lemon grass, using a meat mallet or rolling pin, and add to the saucepan with the Kaffir lime leaves, coriander (cilantro), lime rind and juice, mussels and stock. Put the lid on the saucepan and cook over a medium heat for 3–5 minutes. Shake the saucepan occasionally.

3 Check that the mussels have opened and discard any that remain closed. Lift them out and transfer to 4 warmed soup plates. Boil the remaining liquid rapidly so that it reduces slightly. Remove the lemon grass and kaffir lime leaves, then pour the liquid over the mussels.

4 Garnish with the fresh coriander (cilantro) and lime wedges, and serve with chunks of crusty bread.

Shrimp Rolls

Tasty spring rolls made with shrimps.

SERVES 4

2 tbsp vegetable oil • 3 shallots, chopped very finely
1 carrot, cut into matchsticks
7 cm / 3 inch piece of cucumber, cut into matchsticks
60 g / 2 oz / ½ cup bamboo shoots, shredded finely
125 g / 4 oz / ½ cup peeled (small) shrimps
90 g / 3 oz / ½ cup cooked long-grain rice
1 tbsp fish sauce or light soy sauce • 1 tsp sugar
2 tsp cornflour (cornstarch), blended in 2 tbsp cold water
8   25 cm / 10 inch spring roll wrappers
oil for deep-frying • salt and pepper
Thai plum sauce, to serve

To garnish:

spring onions (scallions) • sprigs of fresh coriander (cilantro)

1 Heat the oil in a wok or frying pan (skillet) and add the shallots, carrot, cucumber and bamboo shoots. Stir-fry briskly for 2–3 minutes. Add the shrimps and rice, and cook for 2 minutes and season.

2 Mix together the fish sauce or soy sauce, sugar and blended cornflour (cornstarch). Add to the stir-fry and cook, stirring constantly, for about 1 minute, until thickened. Leave to cool slightly.

3 Place spoonfuls of the shrimp and vegetable mixture on the spring roll wrappers. Dampen the edges, fold in and roll them up to enclose the filling completely.

4 Heat the oil to 180–190°C/350–375°F or until a cube of bread browns in 30 seconds. Deep-fry the rolls until crisp and drain.

5 Serve garnished with spring onions (scallions) and coriander (cilantro) and accompanied by plum sauce.

Szechuan Prawns (Shrimp)

Use raw prawns (shrimp) if possible, otherwise omit steps 1 and 2 and add the cooked prawns (shrimp) before the sauce at step 3.

SERVES 4

250–300 g/ 8–10 oz raw tiger prawns (jumbo shrimp)
pinch of salt • ½ egg white, lightly beaten
1 tsp Cornflour (Cornstarch) Paste (see page 22)
600 ml/ 1 pint/ 2½ cups vegetable oil
fresh coriander (cilantro) leaves, to garnish

Sauce:
1 tsp finely chopped ginger root
2 spring onions (scallions), chopped finely
1 garlic clove, chopped finely
3–4 small dried red chillies, deseeded and chopped
1 tbsp light soy sauce • 1 tsp rice wine or dry sherry
1 tbsp tomato purée (paste) • 1 tbsp oyster sauce
2–3 tbsp Chinese Stock (see page 24) or water
a few drops of sesame oil

1 Peel the raw prawns (shrimp), then mix with the salt, egg white and cornflour (cornstarch) paste until coated all over.

2 Heat the oil in a preheated wok until it is smoking, then deep-fry the prawns (shrimp) for 1 minute. Remove with a slotted spoon and drain.

3 Pour off the oil, leaving about 1 tablespoon in the wok. Add all the ingredients for the sauce, bring to the boil and stir until smooth and well blended. Add the prawns (shrimp) to the sauce, stirring to blend. Garnish with coriander (cilantro) leaves.

Fried Squid Flowers

The addition of green (bell) pepper and black bean sauce to the squid makes a colourful and delicious dish from the Cantonese school.

SERVES 4

350–400 g/12–13 oz prepared and cleaned squid
1 green (bell) pepper, cored and deseeded
3–4 tbsp vegetable oil
1 garlic clove, chopped finely
¼ tsp finely chopped ginger root
2 tsp finely chopped spring onions (scallions)
½ tsp salt
2 tbsp crushed black bean sauce
1 tsp Chinese rice wine or dry sherry
a few drops of sesame oil

1 Clean the squid by first cutting off the head. Cut off the tentacles and reserve. Remove the small soft bone at the base of the tentacles and the transparent backbone, as well as the ink bag. Peel off the thin skin, then wash and dry thoroughly. Open up the squid and score the inside of the flesh in a criss-cross pattern.

2 Cut the squid into pieces about the size of an oblong postage stamp. Blanch in a bowl of boiling water for a few seconds until all the pieces curl up. Drain and dry thoroughly on paper towels.

3 Cut the (bell) pepper into small triangular pieces. Heat the oil in a preheated wok and stir-fry the (bell) pepper for about 1 minute. Add the garlic, ginger, spring onions (scallions), salt and squid and stir-fry for 1 minute.

4 Finally, add the black bean sauce and wine, and blend well. Serve hot, sprinkled with sesame oil.

Baked Crab with Ginger

**The crab is interchangeable with lobster.
In Chinese restaurants, only live crabs and
lobsters are used, but ready-cooked ones
can be used at home.**

SERVES 4

*1 large or 2 medium crabs,
weighing about 750 g/1½ lb in total
2 tbsp Chinese rice wine or dry sherry
1 egg, lightly beaten
1 tbsp cornflour (cornstarch)
3–4 tbsp vegetable oil
1 tbsp finely chopped ginger root
3–4 spring onions (scallions), cut into sections
2 tbsp light soy sauce
1 tsp sugar
75 ml/3 fl oz/⅓ cup Chinese Stock (see page 24) or water
½ tsp sesame oil
fresh coriander (cilantro) leaves, to garnish*

1 Cut the crab in half from the under-belly. Break off the claws and crack them with the back of a cleaver or large kitchen knife. Discard the legs and crack the shell, breaking it into several pieces. Discard the feathery gills and the stomach sac.

2 Place the crab pieces in a bowl with the wine, egg and cornflour (cornstarch) and leave to marinate for 10–15 minutes.

3 Heat the oil in a preheated wok and stir-fry the crab with the ginger and spring onions (scallions) for 2–3 minutes.

4 Add the soy sauce, sugar and stock or water, blend well and bring to the boil. Cover and cook for 3–4 minutes, then remove the lid. Sprinkle with sesame oil and garnish with fresh coriander (cilantro) leaves before serving.

Spiced Scallops

If using frozen scallops, make sure they are completely defrosted before cooking.

SERVES 4

*12 large scallops with coral attached or 350 g/12 oz small
scallops without coral, defrosted if frozen
4 tbsp sunflower oil
4–6 spring onions (scallions), sliced thinly diagonally
1 garlic clove, crushed
2.5 cm/1 inch piece of ginger root, chopped finely
250 g/8 oz mangetout (snow peas)
125 g/4 oz button or closed cup mushrooms, sliced
2 tbsp sherry • 2 tbsp soy sauce
1 tbsp clear honey • ¼ tsp ground allspice
1 tbsp sesame seeds, toasted • salt and pepper*

1 Rinse and dry the scallops, discarding any black pieces. Detach the corals, if using. Slice each scallop into 3–4 pieces and halve the corals if large.

2 Heat 2 tablespoons of oil in the wok, swirling it around until really hot. Add the spring onions (scallions), garlic and ginger, and stir-fry for 1–2 minutes. Add the mangetout (snow peas) and continue to stir-fry for 2–3 minutes. Transfer to a bowl.

3 Add the remaining oil to the wok. When really hot add the scallops and corals, and stir-fry for 2 minutes. Add the mushrooms and cook for 1–2 minutes.

4 Add the sherry, soy sauce, honey, allspice and salt and pepper to taste. Mix thoroughly, then return the vegetable mixture to the wok.

5 Season well and toss together over a high heat for 1–2 minutes until piping hot. Serve immediately, sprinkled with sesame seeds.

Vegetable Dishes

Through their tradition of vegetarianism, Indian cooks turn the simplest vegetables into the most delicious feasts. Almost all Chinese dishes include vegetables, to give meals a balance of colour, aroma, texture and flavour. When selecting vegetables, always buy crisp, firm specimens, and cook them as soon as possible.

Aubergine (Eggplant) Dipping Platter

Dipping platters are a very sociable dish, bringing together all the diners at the table. This substantial dip is served with vegetables as an appetizer.

SERVES 4

1 aubergine (eggplant), peeled and cut into 2.5 cm/1 inch cubes
3 tbsp sesame seeds, roasted in a dry pan over a low heat
1 tsp sesame oil
grated rind and juice of ½ lime
1 small shallot, diced
½ tsp salt • 1 tsp sugar
1 red chilli, deseeded and sliced • pepper

To serve:
125 g/4 oz broccoli florets • 2 carrots, cut into matchsticks
125 g/4 oz/8 baby sweetcorn cobs, cut in half lengthways
2 celery stalks, cut into matchsticks
1 baby red cabbage, cut into 8 wedges, the leaves of each wedge held together by the core

1 Cook the diced aubergine (eggplant) in boiling water for 7–8 minutes.

2 Meanwhile, grind the sesame seeds with the oil in a food processor or pestle and mortar.

3 Add the aubergine (eggplant), lime rind and juice, shallot, salt, sugar and chilli in that order to the sesame seeds. Process, or chop and mash by hand, until smooth.

4 Adjust the seasoning if necessary then spoon into a bowl. Serve surrounded by the broccoli, carrots, sweetcorn cobs, celery and cabbage.

Sweetcorn Patties

These are a delicious addition to any party buffet, and very simple to prepare. Serve with a sweet chilli sauce.

SERVES 12

325 g/ 11 oz can of sweetcorn, drained
1 onion, chopped finely
1 tsp curry powder
1 garlic clove, crushed
1 tsp ground coriander
2 spring onions (scallions), sliced
3 tbsp plain (all-purpose) flour
½ tsp baking powder
salt
1 large egg
4 tbsp sunflower oil

1 Mash the drained sweetcorn lightly in a medium-sized bowl. Add all the remaining ingredients, except for the sunflower oil, one at a time, stirring after each addition.

2 Heat the oil in a frying pan (skillet). Drop tablespoonfuls of the mixture carefully on to the hot oil, far enough apart for them not to run into each other as they cook.

3 Cook for 4–5 minutes, turning each patty once, until they are golden brown and firm. Take care not to turn them too soon, or they will break up in the pan.

4 Remove from the pan with a spatula or fish slice and drain on paper towels. Serve quickly while still warm.

Paw-paw (Papaya) Salad

Choose firm paw-paws (papayas) for this delicious salad.

SERVES 4

Dressing:

4 tbsp olive oil • 1 tbsp fish sauce or light soy sauce
2 tbsp lime or lemon juice • 1 tbsp dark muscovado sugar
1 tsp finely chopped fresh red or green chilli

Salad:

1 crisp lettuce • ¼ small white cabbage
2 paw-paws (papayas) • 2 tomatoes
30 g/1 oz/¼ cup roast peanuts, chopped roughly
4 spring onions (scallions), trimmed and sliced thinly
basil leaves, to garnish

1 To make the dressing, whisk together the olive oil, fish sauce or soy sauce, lime or lemon juice, sugar and chopped chilli. Set aside, stirring occasionally to dissolve the sugar.

2 Shred the lettuce and cabbage and toss them together. Arrange on a large serving plate.

3 Peel the paw-paws (papayas) and slice them in half. Scoop out the seeds, then slice the flesh thinly. Arrange on top of the shredded lettuce and cabbage.

4 Put the tomatoes into a small bowl and cover them with boiling water. Leave them to stand for 1 minute, then lift them out with a fork and peel them. Remove the seeds and chop the flesh. Arrange them on the salad leaves. Scatter the peanuts and spring onions (scallions) over the top.

5 Whisk the salad dressing to distribute the ingredients and pour over the salad. Garnish with basil leaves and serve at once.

Bamboo Shoots with Cucumber

This simple side dish is the perfect accompaniment to a Thai main meal. Salting the cucumber before it is stir-fried draws out the moisture so that it stays crisp.

SERVES 4

½ cucumber • 2 tbsp sesame oil
4 shallots, chopped finely • 1 garlic clove, sliced finely
350 g/ 12 oz can of bamboo shoots, drained
1 tbsp dry sherry • 1 tbsp soy sauce
2 tsp cornflour (cornstarch) • 1 tsp sesame seeds • salt

To garnish:
2 red chilli flowers • sliced spring onions (scallions)

1 Slice the cucumber thinly and sprinkle with salt. Leave for 10–15 minutes, then rinse with cold water. Meanwhile, to make chilli flowers for garnishing, hold the stem of the chilli and cut down its length several times with a sharp knife. Place in a bowl of chilled water until the 'petals' turn out. Remove the chilli seeds when the 'petals' have opened.

2 Heat the sesame oil in a wok or frying pan (skillet) and add the shallots and garlic. Stir-fry for 2 minutes, until golden. Add the bamboo shoots and cucumber and stir-fry for 2–3 minutes.

3 Blend together the sherry, soy sauce and cornflour (cornstarch). Add to the bamboo shoots and cucumber, stirring to combine. Cook for 1–2 minutes to thicken slightly, then add the sesame seeds and stir them through.

4 Transfer the vegetables to a warmed serving dish. Garnish with the chilli flowers and sliced spring onions (scallions). Serve at once.

Chinese Hot Salad

**A mixture of vegetables stir-fried with a
Chinese flavour, with an added touch of
chilli. To serve cold, add 3–4 tablespoons of
French dressing as the vegetables cool.**

SERVES 4

*1 tbsp dark soy sauce • 1½–2 tsp bottled sweet chilli sauce
2 tbsp sherry • 1 tbsp brown sugar • 1 tbsp wine vinegar
2 tbsp sunflower oil • 1 garlic clove, crushed
4 spring onions (scallions), thinly sliced diagonally
250 g/8 oz courgettes (zucchini), cut into julienne
strips about 4 cm/1½ inches long
250 g/8 oz carrots, cut into julienne strips
about 4 cm/1½ inches long
1 red or green (bell) pepper, cored, deseeded and thinly sliced
1 × 400 g/14 oz can of bean-sprouts, drained
125 g/4 oz French (green) or fine beans,
cut into 5 cm/2 inch lengths
1 tbsp sesame oil • salt and pepper
1–2 tsp sesame seeds, to garnish*

1 Combine the soy sauce, chilli sauce, sherry, sugar, vinegar and salt and pepper to taste.

2 Heat the 2 tablespoons of sunflower oil in a wok, swirling it around until it is really hot. Add the garlic and spring onions (scallions) and stir-fry for 1–2 minutes. Add the courgettes (zucchini), carrots and (bell) peppers and stir-fry for 1–2 minutes, then add the soy sauce mixture and bring to the boil.

3 Add the bean-sprouts and French (green) beans and stir-fry for 1–2 minutes, making sure all the vegetables are coated with the sauce.

4 Drizzle the sesame oil over the vegetables, stir-fry for 30 seconds and serve sprinkled with sesame seeds.

Caraway Cabbage

This makes a delicious vegetable accompaniment to all types of food: it can also be served as a vegetarian main dish.

SERVES 4

500 g/1 lb 2 oz white cabbage
1 tbsp sunflower oil
4 spring onions (scallions), thinly sliced diagonally
60 g/2 oz/½ cup raisins
60 g/2 oz/½ cup walnut pieces or pecan nuts, roughly chopped
5 tbsp milk or vegetable stock
1 tbsp caraway seeds
1–2 tbsp freshly chopped mint
salt and pepper
sprigs of mint, to garnish

1 Remove any outer leaves from the cabbage and cut out the stem. Shred the leaves very finely, either by hand or using the fine slicing blade on a food processor.

2 Heat the oil in a wok, swirling it around until it is really hot. Add the spring onions (scallions) and stir-fry for 1–2 minutes.

3 Add the cabbage and stir-fry for 3–4 minutes, keeping the cabbage moving all the time by stirring from the outside to the centre of the wok. Make sure the cabbage does not go brown.

4 Add the raisins, walnuts and the milk or stock and stir-fry for 3–4 minutes or until the cabbage begins to soften slightly but is still crisp.

5 Season well, add the caraway seeds and 1 tablespoon of the chopped mint and stir-fry for 1–2 minutes. Serve sprinkled with the remaining chopped mint and garnish with sprigs of fresh mint.

Aviyal

This can be served with any type of food, and makes a good vegetarian main dish.

SERVES 4

250 g / 8 oz / 2 ⅔ cups desiccated (shredded) coconut
or 125 g / 4 oz creamed coconut
300 ml / ½ pint / 1¼ cups boiling water • 2 tbsp sunflower oil
30 g / 1 oz piece of ginger root, grated
2 onions, finely chopped • 1 garlic clove, crushed
2 tsp ground coriander • 1 tbsp garam masala
1 tsp turmeric
2 green (bell) peppers, cored, deseeded and sliced in thin rings
1 red or yellow (bell) pepper, cored, deseeded and
sliced in thin rings
2 carrots, cut into julienne strips
1 green chilli pepper, cored, deseeded and sliced (optional)
125–175 g / 4–6 oz French (green) or fine beans,
cut into 7 cm / 3 inch lengths
175 g / 6 oz green broccoli, divided into florets
3 tomatoes, peeled, quartered and deseeded • salt and pepper

1 Soak the coconut in the boiling water for 20 minutes, then process in a food processor until smooth. Alternatively, blend the creamed coconut with the boiling water until smooth.

2 Heat the oil in the wok, swirling it around until really hot. Add the ginger, onions and garlic and stir-fry for 2–3 minutes until they are beginning to colour lightly.

3 Add the coriander, garam masala and turmeric and stir-fry for a few minutes then add the (bell) peppers, carrots, chilli, beans, broccoli and tomatoes, reduce the heat and stir-fry for 4–5 minutes. Add the coconut purée and seasoning and bring to the boil. Stir-fry for 5–8 minutes, until tender but with a bite to the vegetables. Serve as a main dish with rice or noodles, or as a curry accompaniment.

Sweet & Sour Vegetables

Make your choice of vegetables from the suggested list, including spring onions (scallions) and garlic. For a hotter, spicier sauce add chilli sauce.

SERVES 4

5–6 vegetables from the following:
1 (bell) pepper, deseeded and sliced
125 g/ 4 oz French (green) beans, cut into 2–3 pieces
125 g/ 4 oz mangetout (snow peas), cut into 2–3 pieces
250 g/ 8 oz broccoli or cauliflower florets
250 g/ 8 oz courgettes (zucchini), cut into 5 cm/ 2 inch lengths
175 g/ 6 oz carrots, cut into julienne strips
125 g/ 4 oz baby sweetcorn cobs, sliced thinly
175 g/ 6 oz parsnip or celeriac, diced finely
13 celery sticks, sliced thinly crosswise
4 tomatoes, peeled, quartered and deseeded
125 g/ 4 oz button mushrooms, sliced
7 cm/ 3 inch length of cucumber, diced
200 g/ 7 oz can of water chestnuts or bamboo shoots,
drained and sliced
400 g/ 14 oz can of bean-sprouts, drained
4 spring onions (scallions) sliced thinly
2 tbsp sunflower oil • 1 garlic clove, crushed

Sweet & sour sauce:
2 tbsp wine vinegar
2 tbsp clear honey • 1 tbsp tomato purée (paste)
2 tbsp soy sauce • 2 tbsp sherry
1–2 tsp sweet chilli sauce (optional)
2 tsp cornflour (cornstarch)

1 Prepare the selected vegetables, cutting them into uniform lengths.

2 Combine the sauce ingredients in a bowl, blending well together.

3 Heat the oil in the wok, swirling it around until really hot. Add the spring onions (scallions) and garlic and stir-fry for 1 minute.

4 Add the vegetables – the harder and firmer ones first – and stir-fry for 2 minutes. Then add the softer ones such as mushrooms, mangetout (snow peas) and tomatoes and continue to stir-fry for 2 minutes. Add the sweet and sour sauce to the wok. Bring to the boil quickly, tossing until the vegetables are thoroughly coated and the sauce has thickened. Serve hot.

Mixed Bean Stir-Fry

**Any type of canned beans can be used, but
rinse and drain well before use.**

SERVES 4

1 × 400 g/14 oz can of red kidney beans
1 × 400 g/14 oz can of cannellini beans
6 spring onions (scallions)
*1 × 200 g/7 oz can of pineapple rings or pieces in
natural juice, chopped*
2 tbsp pineapple juice • 3–4 pieces stem ginger
2 tbsp ginger syrup from the jar
thinly pared rind of ½ lime or lemon, cut into julienne strips
2 tbsp lime or lemon juice • 2 tbsp soy sauce
1 tsp cornflour (cornstarch) • 1 tbsp sesame oil
*125 g/4 oz French (green) beans,
cut into 4 cm/1½ inch lengths*
1 × 250 g/8 oz can of bamboo shoots, drained and sliced
salt and pepper • rice, to serve (optional)

1 Drain the beans, rinse under cold water and drain again thoroughly. Cut 4 spring onions (scallions) into narrow slanting slices. Thinly slice the remainder and reserve for garnish.

2 Combine the pineapple and juice, ginger and syrup, lime or lemon rind and juice, soy sauce and cornflour (cornstarch).

3 Heat the oil in the wok, swirling it around until really hot. Add the spring onions (scallions) and stir-fry for 1 minute. Add the French (green) beans and bamboo shoots and stir-fry for 2 minutes. Add the pineapple and ginger mixture and bring just to the boil. Add the canned beans and stir until very hot – about 1 minute.

4 Season to taste, and serve with boiled rice sprinkled with the reserved spring onions (scallions); or serve as a vegetable accompaniment.

Gingered Broccoli with Orange

Thinly sliced broccoli florets are lightly stir-fried and served in a ginger and orange sauce.

SERVES 4

750 g/ 1½ lb broccoli
2 thin slices of ginger root
2 garlic cloves
1 orange
2 tsp cornflour (cornstarch)
1 tbsp light soy sauce
½ tsp sugar
2 tbsp vegetable oil

1 Divide the broccoli into small florets. Peel the stems, using a vegetable peeler, and then cut the stems into thin slices. Cut the ginger root into matchsticks and slice the garlic.

2 Peel 2 strips of zest from the orange and cut into strips. Place the strips in a bowl, cover with water and set aside. Squeeze the juice from the orange and mix with the cornflour (cornstarch), soy sauce, sugar and 4 tablespoons of water.

3 Heat the oil in a wok or frying pan (skillet). Add the sliced broccoli stems and stir-fry for 2 minutes. Add the ginger root, garlic and broccoli florets, and stir-fry for 3 minutes.

4 Stir in the orange sauce mixture and cook, stirring constantly, until the sauce has thickened and coated the broccoli. Drain the reserved orange zest and stir into the wok or pan before serving.

Braised Chinese Leaves

White cabbage can be used instead of Chinese leaves for this dish. Try to use the correct type of peppercorns in preparing the recipe. Szechuan red peppercorns have a pungent, aromatic odour which distinguishes them from the hotter black peppercorns. Roast them briefly in the oven or sauté them in a dry frying pan (skillet), then grind them in a spice grinder or pestle and mortar and store in a jar until needed.

SERVES 4

500 g/1 lb 2 oz Chinese leaves or firm white cabbage
3 tbsp vegetable oil
½ tsp Szechuan peppercorns
5–6 small dried red chillies, deseeded and chopped
½ tsp salt
1 tbsp sugar
1 tbsp light soy sauce
1 tbsp rice vinegar
a few drops of sesame oil (optional)

1 Shred the Chinese leaves or cabbage crossways into thin pieces. (If using firm-packed white cabbage, cut out and discard the thick core before shredding the leaves.)

2 Heat the oil in a preheated wok, add the Szechuan peppercorns and the dried chillies and stir-fry for a few seconds.

3 Add the Chinese leaves or white cabbage to the peppercorns and chillies, stir-fry for about 1 minute, then add the salt and continue stir-frying for 1 minute.

4 Add the sugar, soy sauce and vinegar, blend well and stir-fry for 1 minute. Sprinkle with the sesame oil, if using. Serve hot or cold.

Garlicky Mushroom Pakoras

Whole button mushrooms are dunked in a spiced garlicky batter and deep fried until golden.

SERVES 6

175 g/6 oz/1½ cups gram flour • ½ tsp salt
¼ tsp baking powder • 1 tsp cumin seeds
½–1 tsp chilli powder, to taste
200 ml/7 fl oz/¾ cup water
2 garlic cloves, crushed • 1 small onion, finely chopped
vegetable oil, for deep frying
500 g/1 lb 2 oz button mushrooms, trimmed and wiped

To garnish:
lemon wedges • sprigs of coriander (cilantro)

1 Put the gram flour, salt, baking powder, cumin and chilli powder into a bowl and mix together. Make a well in the centre and gradually stir in the water, to form a batter.

2 Stir the crushed garlic and the chopped onion into the batter and leave the mixture to infuse for 10 minutes. One-third fill a deep-fat fryer with vegetable oil and heat to 180°C/350°F or until a cube of day-old bread is browned in 30 seconds. Lower the basket into the oil.

3 Meanwhile, mix the mushrooms into the batter, stirring to coat. Remove a few at a time and place them into the hot oil. Fry for about 2 minutes or until golden brown.

4 Remove from the pan with a slotted spoon and drain on paper towels while cooking the remainder in the same way. Serve hot, sprinkled with coarse salt and garnished with lemon wedges and sprigs of coriander (cilantro).

Curried Okra

Okra, also known as bhindi and ladies' fingers, are a favourite Indian vegetable. They are now widely available.

SERVES 4

500 g/1 lb 2 oz fresh okra
4 tbsp vegetable ghee or oil
1 bunch spring onions (scallions), trimmed and sliced
2 garlic cloves, crushed
5 cm/2 inch piece of ginger root, chopped finely
1 tsp minced chilli (from a jar)
1½ tsp ground cumin
1 tsp ground coriander
1 tsp ground turmeric
200 g/7 oz can of chopped tomatoes
150 ml/¼ pint/⅔ cup vegetable stock
1 tsp Garam Masala (see page 9)
salt and pepper
chopped fresh coriander (cilantro), to garnish

1 Rinse the okra, trim off the stalks and pat dry.

2 Heat the ghee or oil in a large pan, add the spring onions (scallions), garlic, ginger and chilli and fry gently for 1 minute, stirring frequently.

3 Stir in the ground cumin, coriander and turmeric and fry gently for 30 seconds, then add the tomatoes, stock and okra. Season with salt and pepper to taste and simmer for about 15 minutes, stirring and turning the mixture occasionally. The okra should be cooked but still a little crisp.

4 Sprinkle with the garam masala, taste and adjust the seasoning, if necessary.

5 Garnish with the chopped coriander (cilantro) and serve hot.

Aubergine (Eggplant) in Saffron Sauce

Here is a quick and simple, delicately spiced and delicious way to cook aubergine (eggplant).

SERVES 4

a good pinch of saffron strands, crushed
1 tbsp boiling water
1 large aubergine (eggplant)
3 tbsp vegetable oil
1 large onion, coarsely chopped
2 garlic cloves, crushed
2.5 cm/1 inch piece of ginger root, chopped
1½ tbsp mild or medium curry paste
1 tsp cumin seeds
150 ml/¼ pint/⅔ cup double (heavy) cream
150 ml/¼ pint/⅔ cup strained thick yogurt
2 tbsp mango chutney, chopped if necessary
salt and pepper

1 Place the saffron in a small bowl, add the boiling water and leave to infuse for at least 5 minutes.

2 Trim the leaf end off the aubergine (eggplant), cut lengthways into quarters, then into 1 cm/½ inch thick slices.

3 Heat the oil in a large frying pan (skillet), add the onion and cook gently for 3 minutes. Stir in the aubergine (eggplant), garlic, ginger, curry paste and cumin, and cook gently for 3 minutes.

4 Stir in the saffron solution, cream, yogurt and chutney, and cook gently for 8–10 minutes, stirring frequently, until the aubergine (eggplant) is cooked through and tender. Season with salt and pepper to taste and serve hot.

Fried Spiced Potatoes

A deliciously good accompaniment to almost any main course dish.

SERVES 4

2 onions, chopped coarsely
5 cm/2 inch piece of ginger root, chopped • 2 garlic cloves
2–3 tbsp mild or medium curry paste
4 tbsp water • 750 g/1½ lb new potatoes
vegetable oil, for deep frying
3 tbsp vegetable ghee or oil
150 ml/¼ pint/⅔ cup strained thick yogurt
150 ml/¼ pint/⅔ cup double (heavy) cream
3 tbsp chopped fresh mint • salt and pepper
spring onions (scallions), trimmed and sliced, to garnish

1 Place the onions, ginger, garlic, curry paste and water in a blender or food processor and process until smooth.

2 Cut the potatoes into quarters – the pieces need to be about 2.5 cm/1 inch in size – and pat dry with paper towels.

3 Heat the oil in a deep-fat fryer to 180°C/350°F and fry the potatoes, in batches, for about 5 minutes or until golden brown, turning frequently. Remove from the pan and drain on paper towels.

4 Heat the ghee or oil in a large frying pan (skillet), add the onion mixture and fry gently for 2 minutes, stirring all the time. Add the yogurt, cream and 2 tablespoons of the mint and mix well.

5 Add the fried potatoes and stir until coated in the sauce. Cook for a further 5–7 minutes or until heated through and the sauce has thickened, stirring frequently. Season with salt and pepper to taste and sprinkle with the remaining mint and sliced spring onions (scallions). Serve immediately.

Kashmiri Spinach

This is an imaginative way to serve spinach, which adds a little zip to it. It is a very simple dish, and will complement almost any curry.

SERVES 4

500g/ 1 lb 2 oz spinach (Swiss chard or baby leaf spinach may be substituted)
2 tbsp mustard oil
¼ tsp Garam Masala (see page 9)
1 tsp yellow mustard seeds
2 spring onions (scallions), sliced

1 Remove the tough stalks from the spinach.

2 Heat the mustard oil in a wok or large heavy frying pan (skillet) until it smokes. Add the garam masala and mustard seeds. Cover the pan quickly – you will hear the mustard seeds popping inside.

3 When the popping has ceased, remove the cover, add the spring onions (scallions) and stir in the spinach until wilted.

4 Continue cooking the spinach, uncovered, over a medium heat for 10–15 minutes, until most of the water has evaporated. If using frozen spinach, it will not need as much cooking – cook it until most of the water has evaporated.

5 Remove the spinach and spring onions (scallions) with a perforated spoon in order to drain off any remaining liquid. This dish is more pleasant to eat when it is served as dry as possible. Serve immediately while it is piping hot.

Rice, Noodles, Pulses, Breads

Rice is a staple ingredient in India and southern China. However, in northern China where wheat grows abundantly, noodles are the mainstay of everyday eating, as they are in Thailand. Indian breads are also featured and they make delicious accompaniments to the main dishes of the previous chapters.

Egg Fried Rice

**The rice used for frying should not
be too soft. Ideally, the rice should have
been slightly under-cooked and left
to cool before frying.**

SERVES 4

3 eggs
1 tsp salt
2 spring onions (scallions), finely chopped
2–3 tbsp vegetable oil
500 g/ 1 lb 2 oz/ 3 cups cooked rice,
well drained and cooled (see note in step 3)
125 g/ 4 oz cooked peas

1 Lightly beat the eggs with a pinch of salt and 1 tablespoon of the spring onions (scallions).

2 Heat the oil in a preheated wok, add the eggs and stir until lightly scrambled. (The eggs should only be cooked until they start to set, so they are still moist.)

3 Add the rice and stir to make sure that each grain of rice is separated. Note: the cooked rice should be cool, preferably cold, so that much of the moisture has evaporated. This ensures that the oil will coat the grains of rice and prevent them sticking. Store the cooked rice in the refrigerator until ready to cook. Make sure the oil is really hot before adding the rice, to avoid the rice being saturated with oil, which will make it heavy and greasy.

4 Add the remaining salt, spring onions (scallions) and peas to the wok. Blend well and serve hot or cold.

Egg Fu-Yung with Rice

**This dish is a great way of using up
leftover cooked rice. It can be served as a
meal by itself or as an accompaniment.**

SERVES 2–4

175 g / 6 oz / ³⁄₄ cup long-grain rice
*2 Chinese dried mushrooms (if unavailable, use thinly sliced
open-cup mushrooms)*
3 eggs, beaten • 3 tbsp vegetable oil
4 spring onions (scallions), sliced
½ green (bell) pepper, chopped
60 g / 2 oz / ⅓ cup canned bamboo shoots
60 g / 2 oz / ⅓ cup canned water chestnuts, sliced
125 g / 4 oz / 2 cups bean-sprouts
2 tbsp light soy sauce • 2 tbsp dry sherry
2 tsp sesame oil • salt and pepper

1 Cook the rice in lightly salted boiling water according to the instructions on the packet.

2 Place the dried mushrooms in a small bowl, cover with warm water and leave to soak for 20–25 minutes.

3 Mix the beaten eggs with a pinch of salt. Heat 1 tablespoon of the oil in a wok or large frying pan (skillet). Add the eggs and stir until just set. Remove and set aside.

4 Drain the mushrooms and squeeze out the excess water. Remove the tough centres and discard. Slice the mushrooms thinly.

5 Heat the remaining oil in a clean wok or frying pan (skillet). Add the mushrooms, spring onions (scallions) and green (bell) pepper, and stir-fry for 2 minutes. Add the bamboo shoots, water chestnuts and bean-sprouts. Stir-fry for 1 minute.

6 Drain the rice thoroughly and add to the pan with

the soy sauce, dry sherry and
sesame oil. Mix well, heating
the rice thoroughly. Season to
taste with salt and pepper.
Stir in the reserved eggs and
serve hot.

Fragrant Steamed Rice in Lotus Leaves

The fragrance of the lotus leaves penetrates the rice, giving it a unique taste.

SERVES 4

2 lotus leaves (if unavailable, use large cabbage or spinach leaves)
4 Chinese dried mushrooms (if unavailable, use thinly sliced open-cup mushrooms)
175 g / 6 oz / ³⁄₄ cup long-grain rice • 1 cinnamon stick
6 cardamom pods • 4 cloves
1 tsp salt • 2 eggs • 1 tbsp vegetable oil
2 spring onions (scallions), chopped • 1 tbsp soy sauce
2 tbsp sherry • 1 tsp sugar • 1 tsp sesame oil

1 Unfold the lotus leaves carefully and cut along the fold to divide each leaf in half. Lay on a large baking sheet (cookie sheet) and pour over enough hot water to cover. Leave to soak for about 30 minutes or until the leaves have softened.

2 Place the dried mushrooms in a small bowl and cover with warm water. Leave to soak for 20–25 minutes.

3 Cook the rice in a saucepan of boiling water with the cinnamon stick, cardamom pods, cloves and salt for about 10 minutes – the rice should be partially cooked. Drain well and remove the cinnamon stick.

4 Beat the eggs lightly. Heat the oil in a wok or frying pan (skillet) and cook the eggs quickly, stirring until set; then remove and set aside.

5 Drain the mushrooms, squeezing out the excess water. Remove the tough centres and discard, and chop the mushrooms. Place the drained rice in a bowl. Stir in the mushrooms, cooked egg,

spring onions (scallions), soy sauce, sherry, sugar and sesame oil. Season with salt.

6 Drain the lotus leaves and divide the rice mixture into 4 portions. Place a portion in the centre of each lotus leaf and fold up to form a parcel (package). Place in a steamer, cover and steam over simmering water for 20 minutes. To serve, cut the tops of the lotus leaves open to expose the fragrant rice inside.

Nasi Goreng

An Indonesian rice dish flavoured with vegetables, pork, soy sauce and curry spices.

SERVES 4

300 g/ 10 oz/ 1½ cups long-grain rice
350–500 g/ 12 oz–1 lb pork fillet or lean pork slices
3 tomatoes, peeled, quartered and deseeded
2 eggs • 4 tsp water • 3 tbsp sunflower oil
1 onion, thinly sliced • 1–2 garlic cloves, crushed
1 tsp medium or mild curry powder • ½ tsp ground coriander
¼ tsp medium chilli powder or 1 tsp bottled sweet chilli sauce
2 tbsp soy sauce • 125 g/ 4 oz frozen peas, defrosted
salt and pepper

1 Cook the rice in boiling salted water, following the instructions given in Chinese Fried Rice (see page 196) and keep warm.

2 Meanwhile, cut the pork into narrow strips across the grain, discarding any fat. Slice the tomatoes.

3 Beat each egg separately with 2 teaspoons of cold water and salt and pepper. Heat 2 teaspoons of oil in the wok, swirling it around until really hot. Pour in the first egg, swirl it around and cook undisturbed until set. Transfer to a plate and repeat with the second egg. Cut the omelettes into strips about 1 cm/½ inch wide.

4 Heat the remaining oil in the wok and when really hot add the onion and garlic and stir-fry for 1–2 minutes. Add the pork and stir-fry for 3 minutes or until almost cooked. Add the curry powder, coriander, chilli powder or chilli sauce and soy sauce and cook for 1 minute, stirring constantly. Stir in the rice, tomatoes and peas and stir-fry for about 2 minutes until hot. Adjust the seasoning and turn into a heated serving dish. Arrange the strips of omelette on top and serve.

Rice with Crab & Mussels

Mussels and crab add flavour and texture to this spicy dish.

SERVES 4, OR 6 AS A STARTER

300 g/ 10 oz/ 1½ cups long-grain rice
175 g/ 6 oz crab meat, fresh, canned or frozen
(defrosted if frozen), or 8 crab sticks, defrosted if frozen
2 tbsp sesame or sunflower oil
2.5 cm/ 1 inch piece of ginger root, grated
4 spring onions (scallions), thinly sliced diagonally
125 g/ 4 oz mangetout (snow peas), cut into 2–3 pieces
½ tsp turmeric • 1 tsp ground cumin
2 × 200 g/ 7 oz jars of mussels, well drained,
or 350 g/ 12 oz frozen mussels, defrosted
1 × 400 g/ 14 oz can of bean-sprouts, well drained
salt and pepper

To garnish:
crab claws or legs • 8 mangetout (snow peas), blanched

1 Cook the rice in boiling salted water, following the instructions given in Chinese Fried Rice (see page 196).

2 Extract the crab meat, if using fresh crab. Flake the crab meat or cut the crab sticks into 3 or 4 pieces.

3 Heat the oil in the wok, swirling it around until really hot. Add the ginger and spring onions (scallions) and stir-fry for 1 minute. Add the mangetout (snow peas) and cook for 1 minute. Sprinkle the turmeric, cumin and seasoning over the vegetables and mix well. Add the crab meat and mussels and stir-fry for 1 minute.

4 Stir in the cooked rice and bean-sprouts and stir-fry for 2 minutes or until hot and well mixed. Adjust the seasoning and serve very hot, garnished with crab claws and mangetout (snow peas).

Coconut Rice

**A pale yellow rice flavoured with coconut
and spices to serve as an accompaniment –
or as a main dish with added diced meat.**

SERVES 4

90 g/3 oz creamed coconut
750 ml/1¼ pints/3 cups boiling water
1 tbsp sunflower oil (or olive oil for a stronger flavour)
1 onion, thinly sliced or chopped
250 g/8 oz/1¼ cups long-grain rice • ¼ tsp turmeric
6 whole cloves • 1 cinnamon stick • ½ tsp salt
60–90 g/2–3 oz/½ cup raisins or sultanas (golden raisins)
60 g/2 oz/½ cup walnut or pecan halves, roughly chopped
2 tbsp pumpkin seeds (optional)
watercress sprigs, to garnish (optional)

1 Blend the creamed coconut with half the boiling water until smooth, then mix in the remainder and stir until well blended.

2 Heat the oil in the wok, add the onion and stir-fry gently for 3–4 minutes until the onion begins to soften but not brown.

3 Rinse the rice under cold running water, drain well and add to the wok with the turmeric. Cook for 1–2 minutes, stirring all the time. Add the coconut mixture, cloves, cinnamon stick and salt and bring to the boil. Cover with the wok lid, or a lid made of foil, and simmer very gently for 10 minutes.

4 Add the raisins, nuts and pumpkin seeds, if using, and mix well. Cover the wok again and cook for 5–8 minutes or until all the liquid has been absorbed and the rice is tender. Remove from the heat and leave to stand, still covered, for 5 minutes before serving. Remove the cinnamon stick. Serve garnished with watercress sprigs, if liked.

Fried Rice with Prawns (Shrimp)

Use either large peeled prawns (shrimp) or tiger prawns (shrimp) for this rice dish.

SERVES 4

300 g/ 10 oz/ 1½ cups long-grain rice • 2 eggs
4 tsp cold water • 3 tbsp sunflower oil
4 spring onions (scallions), thinly sliced diagonally
1 garlic clove, crushed
125 g/ 4 oz closed cup or button mushrooms, thinly sliced
2 tbsp oyster or anchovy sauce
1 × 200 g/ 7 oz can of water chestnuts, drained and sliced
250 g/ 8 oz peeled prawns (shrimp), defrosted if frozen
½ bunch of watercress, roughly chopped
salt and pepper

1 Cook the rice in boiling salted water, following the instructions given in Chinese Fried Rice (see page 196) and keep warm.

2 Beat each egg separately with 2 teaspoons of cold water and salt and pepper. Heat 2 teaspoons of oil in a wok, swirling it around until really hot. Pour in the first egg, swirl it around and leave to cook undisturbed until set. Remove to a plate or board and repeat with the second egg. Cut the omelettes into 2.5 cm/ 1 inch squares.

3 Heat the remaining oil in the wok and when really hot add the spring onions (scallions) and garlic and stir-fry for 1 minute. Add the mushrooms and cook for 2 minutes. Stir in the oyster or anchovy sauce and seasoning and add the water chestnuts and prawns (shrimp); stir-fry for 2 minutes.

4 Stir in the cooked rice and stir-fry for 1 minute, then add the watercress and omelette squares and stir-fry for 1–2 minutes until hot. Serve at once.

Chinese Fried Rice

It is essential to use cold, dry rice with separate grains to make this dish properly.

SERVES 4, OR 6 AS AN ACCOMPANIMENT

750 ml/1¼ pints/3 cups water • ½ tsp salt
300 g/10 oz/1½ cups long-grain rice
2 eggs • 4 tsp cold water • 3 tbsp sunflower oil
4 spring onions (scallions), sliced diagonally
1 red, green or yellow (bell) pepper, cored,
deseeded and thinly sliced
3–4 lean rashers of bacon, rinded and cut into strips
200 g/7 oz fresh bean-sprouts
125 g/4 oz frozen peas, defrosted
2 tbsp soy sauce (optional) • salt and pepper

1 Pour the water into the wok with the salt and bring to the boil. Rinse the rice in a sieve under cold water until the water runs clear, drain well and add to the boiling water. Stir well, then cover the wok tightly with the lid or a lid made of foil, and simmer gently for 12–13 minutes, (do not remove the lid during cooking). Remove the lid, give the rice a good stir and spread out on a large plate or baking (cookie) sheet to cool and dry.

2 Beat each egg separately with salt and pepper and 2 teaspoons of cold water. Heat 1 tablespoon of oil in the wok, swirling it around until hot. Pour in the first egg, swirl it around and leave to cook until set. Remove to a board or plate; repeat with the second egg. Cut the omelettes into thin slices.

3 Add the remaining oil to the wok and when really hot add the spring onions (scallions) and (bell) pepper and stir-fry for 1–2 minutes. Add the bacon and stir-fry for 1–2 minutes. Add the bean-sprouts and peas and toss together; stir in the soy sauce, if using.

4 Add the cooked rice and seasoning and stir-fry for 1–2 minutes, then add the strips of omelette and continue to stir for about 2 minutes or until the rice is piping hot. Serve at once.

Thai Jasmine Rice

Every Thai meal has as its centrepiece a big bowl of steaming, fluffy Thai jasmine rice. The method used for cooking rice in Thailand is the absorption method, but the open pan method is also given below, as this is the one most familiar to Western cooks. Salt should not be added.

SERVES 3–4

Open pan method:
250 g/ 8 oz/ 1¼ cups Thai jasmine rice
1 litre/ 1¾ pints water

1 Rinse the rice in a sieve (strainer) under cold running water and leave to drain thoroughly.

2 Bring the water to the boil. Add the rice, stir and cook over a medium heat, uncovered, for 8–10 minutes.

3 Drain the rice and fork through lightly before serving.

Absorption method:
250 g/ 8 oz/ 1¼ cups Thai jasmine rice
450 ml/ ¾ pint water

1 Rinse the rice in a sieve (strainer) under cold running water.

2 Put the rice and water into a saucepan and bring to the boil. Stir once and then cover the pan tightly with the pan lid or a piece of foil. Lower the heat as much as possible and cook for 10 minutes. Leave to rest for 5 minutes, then fork through lightly and serve hot.

Green Rice

A deliciously different way to serve plain rice for a special occasion or to liven up a simple meal

SERVES 4

2 tbsp olive oil
500 g / 1 lb 2 oz / 2¼ cups basmati or Thai jasmine rice, soaked for 1 hour, washed and drained
750 ml / 1¼ pints / 3 cups coconut milk
1 tsp salt
1 bay leaf
2 tbsp chopped fresh coriander (cilantro)
2 tbsp chopped fresh mint
2 green chillies, deseeded and chopped finely
lime wedges, to garnish

1 Heat the oil in a saucepan, add the rice and stir until it becomes translucent.

2 Add the coconut milk, salt and bay leaf to the pan. Bring to the boil and cook until all the liquid is absorbed.

3 Lower the heat as much as possible, cover the saucepan tightly with the lid or a piece of foil and cook for 10 minutes. Remove the bay leaf.

4 Stir in the chopped coriander (cilantro), mint and green chillies. Fork through the rice gently and serve immediately, garnished with lime wedges.

Chatuchak Fried Rice

**An excellent way to use up leftover rice.
Pop it in the freezer as soon as it is cool,
and it will be ready to reheat at any time.**

SERVES 4

*1 tbsp sunflower oil • 3 shallots, chopped finely
2 garlic cloves, crushed
1 red chilli, deseeded and chopped finely
2.5 cm/1 inch piece of ginger root, shredded finely
½ green (bell) pepper, deseeded and sliced finely
150 g/5 oz/2–3 baby aubergines (eggplants), quartered
90 g/3 oz sugar snap peas or mangetout
(snow peas), trimmed and blanched
90 g/3 oz/6 baby sweetcorn cobs, halved lengthways
and blanched
1 tomato, cut into 8 pieces • 90 g/3 oz/1½ cups bean-sprouts
500 g/1 lb 2 oz/2¼ cups cooked Thai jasmine rice
2 tbsp tomato ketchup • 2 tbsp light soy sauce
fresh coriander (cilantro) leaves and lime wedges, to garnish*

1 Heat the oil in a wok or large, heavy frying pan (skillet) over a high heat. Add the shallots, garlic, chilli and ginger. Stir until the shallots have softened.

2 Add the green (bell) pepper and baby aubergines (eggplants) and stir. Add the sugar snap peas or mangetout (snow peas), baby sweetcorn, tomato and bean-sprouts. Stir for 3 minutes.

3 Add the rice, and lift and stir with 2 spoons for 4–5 minutes, until no more steam is released. Stir in the tomato ketchup and light soy sauce.

4 Serve immediately, garnished with coriander (cilantro) leaves and lime wedges to squeeze over the rice.

Massaman Curried Rice

Massaman paste is the mildest Thai curry paste, and makes a deliciously rich curry.

SERVES 4

Paste:

1 tsp coriander seeds • 1 tsp cumin seeds
1 tsp ground cinnamon • 1 tsp cloves • 1 whole star anise
1 tsp cardamom pods • 1 tsp white peppercorns
1 tbsp oil • 6 shallots, chopped very roughly
6 garlic cloves, chopped very roughly
5 cm/ 2 inch piece of lemon grass, sliced
4 fresh red chillies, deseeded and chopped
grated rind of 1 lime • 1 tsp salt
1 tbsp chopped roast peanuts to garnish

Curry:

3 tbsp sunflower oil
250 g/ 8 oz marinated tofu (bean curd),
cut into 2.5 cm/ 1 inch cubes
125 g/ 4 oz green beans, cut into 2.5cm/ 1 inch lengths
1 kg/ 2 lb/ 6 cups cooked rice (300 g/ 10 oz/ 1½ cups
raw weight)
3 shallots, diced finely and deep-fried
1 spring onion (scallion), chopped finely
2 tbsp chopped roast peanuts • 1 tbsp lime juice

1 To make the paste grind together the spices in a pestle and mortar or spice grinder. Heat the oil in a saucepan and add the shallots, garlic and lemon grass. Cook over a low heat for 5 minutes until soft, then add the chillies and grind with the dry spices. Stir in the lime rind and salt.

2 To make the curry, heat the oil in a wok or large, heavy frying pan (skillet). Cook the tofu (bean curd) over a high heat for 2 minutes to seal. Add the

paste and beans, and stir.
Add the cooked rice and,
using 2 spoons, lift and stir
over a high heat for about
3 minutes.

3 Transfer to a warmed
serving dish. Sprinkle with
the deep-fried shallots, spring
onions (scallions) and peanuts.
Sprinkle over the lime juice.

Spiced Basmati Pilau

**Omit the broccoli and mushrooms if you
want a simple spiced pilau. Remove the
whole spices before serving.**

SERVES 6

*500 g / 1 lb 2 oz / 2½ cups basmati rice
175 g / 6 oz broccoli • 6 tbsp vegetable oil
2 large onions, chopped
250 g / 8 oz mushrooms, wiped and sliced
2 garlic cloves, crushed • 6 cardamom pods, split
6 whole cloves • 8 black peppercorns
1 cinnamon stick or piece of cassia bark
1 tsp ground turmeric
1.25 litres / 2¼ pints / 5 cups boiling vegetable stock or water
60 g / 2 oz / ⅓ cup seedless raisins
60 g / 2 oz / ½ cup unsalted pistachios, coarsely chopped
salt and pepper*

1 Place the rice in a sieve and rinse under cold running water until the water runs clear. Drain. Trim off the broccoli stalk and cut into florets, then quarter the stalk lengthways and cut diagonally into 1 cm / ½ inch pieces.

2 Heat the oil in a large saucepan, add the onions and broccoli stalks and cook for 3 minutes, stirring often. Add the mushrooms, rice, garlic and spices and cook for 1 minute, stirring often until the rice is coated in oil.

3 Add the boiling stock and season with salt and pepper. Stir in the broccoli florets and bring the mixture back to the boil. Cover, reduce the heat and cook gently for 15 minutes.

4 Remove from the heat and leave to stand for 5 minutes, covered. Add the raisins and pistachios and gently fork through to fluff up the grains. Serve hot.

Seafood Chow Mein

Use any seafood available for this delicious dish – mussels or crab would be suitable.

SERVES 4

90 g / 3 oz squid, cleaned • 3–4 fresh scallops
90 g / 3 oz raw prawns (shrimp), shelled
½ egg white, beaten lightly
1 tbsp Cornflour (Cornstarch) Paste (see page 22)
275 g / 9 oz egg noodles • 5–6 tbsp vegetable oil
2 tbsp light soy sauce • 60 g / 2 oz mangetout (snow peas)
½ tsp salt • ½ tsp sugar
1 tsp Chinese rice wine or dry sherry
2 spring onions (scallions), shredded finely
a few drops of sesame oil

1 Open up the squid and score the inside in a criss-cross pattern. Cut into pieces about the size of a postage stamp. Soak the squid in a bowl of boiling water until all the pieces curl up. Rinse in cold water and drain.

2 Cut each scallop into 3–4 slices. Cut the prawns (shrimp) in half lengthways if large. Mix the scallops and prawns with the egg white and cornflour (cornstarch) paste.

3 Cook the noodles in boiling water according to the instructions on the packet, then drain and rinse under cold water. Drain well, then toss with 1 tablespoon of oil.

4 Heat 3 tablespoons of oil in a preheated wok. Add the noodles and 1 tablespoon of the soy sauce and stir-fry for 2–3 minutes. Remove to a serving dish and keep warm.

5 Heat the remaining oil in the wok and add the mangetout (snow peas) and seafood. Stir-fry for about 2 minutes, then add the salt, sugar, wine, remaining soy sauce and about half the spring onions (scallions). Blend well and add a little stock or water if necessary.

6 Pour the seafood mixture on top of the noodles and sprinkle with sesame oil.

Garnish with the remaining spring onions (scallions) and serve hot or cold.

Singapore-Style Rice Noodles

Rice noodles, or vermicelli, are also known as rice sticks. Egg noodles can be used for this dish, but it will not taste quite the same.

SERVES 4

200 g/ 7 oz rice vermicelli
125 g/ 4 oz cooked chicken or pork
60 g/ 2 oz peeled prawns (shrimp), defrosted if frozen
4 tbsp vegetable oil
1 onion, shredded thinly
125 g/ 4 oz/ 2 cups fresh bean-sprouts
1 tsp salt
1 tbsp mild curry powder
2 tbsp light soy sauce
2 spring onions (scallions), shredded thinly
1–2 small fresh green or red chilli peppers, deseeded and shredded thinly

1 Soak the rice vermicelli in boiling water for 8–10 minutes, then rinse in cold water and drain well.

2 Thinly slice the cooked meat. Dry the prawns (shrimp) on paper towels.

3 Heat the oil in a preheated wok. Add the onion and stir-fry until opaque. Add the bean-sprouts and stir-fry for 1 minute.

4 Add the noodles with the meat and prawns (shrimp), and continue stir-frying for 1 minute.

5 Blend in the salt, curry powder and soy sauce, followed by the spring onions (scallions) and chilli peppers. Stir-fry for 1 minute, then serve immediately.

Yellow Split Pea Casserole

If ever there was a winter warmer, this is it – satisfying, and ideal for serving with a lightweight dish such as pilau or biryani.

Serves 4

2 tbsp ghee • 1 tsp black mustard seeds
1 onion, chopped finely • 2 garlic cloves, crushed
1 carrot, grated • 2.5 cm/1 inch piece of ginger root, grated
1 green chilli, deseeded and chopped finely
1 tbsp tomato purée (paste)
250 g/8 oz/1 cup yellow split peas, soaked in
water for 2 hours and drained
400 g/14 oz can of chopped tomatoes
500 ml/16 fl oz/2 cups vegetable stock
250 g/8 oz/1½ cups pumpkin, cubed
250 g/8 oz cauliflower, cut into florets • 2 tbsp oil
1 large aubergine (eggplant), cubed
1 tbsp chopped fresh coriander (cilantro)
1 tsp Garam Masala (see page 9) • salt and pepper

1 Melt the ghee over a medium heat in a large pan. Add the mustard seeds, and when they start to splutter, add the onion, garlic, carrot, and ginger. Cook until soft, about 5 minutes. Add the chilli and stir in the tomato purée (paste). Stir in the split peas. Add the tomatoes and stock, and bring to the boil. Season well. Simmer for 40 minutes, stirring occasionally. Add the pumpkin and cauliflower, and simmer for a further 30 minutes, covered, until the split peas are soft.

2 Meanwhile, heat the oil in a frying pan (skillet) over a high heat. Add the aubergine (eggplant), and stir until sealed on all sides. Remove and drain on paper towels.

3 Stir the aubergine (eggplant) into the split pea mixture with the

coriander (cilantro) and
garam masala.

4 Transfer to a serving dish
and serve immediately.

Channa Dal

This is a dish to consider next time you prepare a dal. Many types of dal (dried pulses and lentils) are used in India – yellow split peas is just one.

SERVES 4

2 tbsp ghee • 1 large onion, chopped finely
1 garlic clove, crushed • 1 tbsp grated ginger root
1 tbsp cumin seeds, ground • 1 dried red chilli
2 tsp coriander seeds, ground
2.5 cm/1 inch piece cinnamon stick
1 tsp salt
½ tsp ground turmeric
250 g/½ lb/2 cups yellow split peas,
soaked in cold water for 1 hour and drained
400 g/14 oz can of plum tomatoes
300 ml/½ pint/1¼ cups water
2 tsp Garam Masala (see page 9)

1 Heat the ghee in a large saucepan, add the onion, garlic and ginger and fry for 3–4 minutes until the onion has softened slightly.

2 Add the cumin, chilli, coriander, cinnamon, salt and turmeric, then stir in the split peas and mix well.

3 Add the tomatoes, breaking them up slightly with the back of a wooden spoon.

4 Add the water and bring to the boil. Reduce the heat to very low and simmer, uncovered, for about 40 minutes, stirring occasionally, until most of the liquid has been absorbed and the split peas are tender. Skim the surface occasionally with a perforated spoon to remove any scum.

5 Gradually stir in the garam masala, tasting after each addition, until it is of the required flavour.

Brindil Bhaji

This is one of the most delicious of the bhaji dishes, and has a wonderful sweet spicy flavour.

SERVES 4

500 g/1 lb 2 oz aubergines (eggplant),
cut into 1 cm/½ inch slices
2 tbsp ghee
1 onion, sliced thinly
2 garlic cloves, sliced thinly
2.5 cm/1 inch piece of ginger root, grated
½ tsp ground turmeric
1 dried red chilli
½ tsp salt
400 g/14 oz can of tomatoes
1 tsp Garam Masala (see page 9)
sprigs of fresh coriander (cilantro), to garnish

1 Cut the aubergine (eggplant) slices into finger-width strips using a sharp knife.

2 Heat the ghee in a saucepan and cook the onion over a medium heat for 7–8 minutes, stirring constantly, until very soft.

3 Add the garlic and aubergine (eggplant), increase the heat and cook for 2 minutes.

4 Stir in the ginger, turmeric, chilli, salt and the tomatoes. Use the back of a wooden spoon to break up the tomatoes. Simmer uncovered for 15–20 minutes until the aubergine (eggplant) is very soft.

5 Stir in the garam masala and simmer for a further 4–5 minutes.

6 Serve garnished with sprigs of fresh coriander (cilantro).

Muttar Paneer

Paneer is a delicious fresh, soft cheese frequently used in Indian cooking.

SERVES 4

150 ml/¼ pint/⅔ cup vegetable oil
2 onions, chopped • 2 garlic cloves, crushed
2.5 cm/1 inch piece of ginger root, chopped finely
1 tsp Garam Masala (see page 9) • 1 tsp ground turmeric
1 tsp chilli powder • 500 g/1 lb 2 oz frozen peas
200 g/7 oz can of chopped tomatoes
120 ml/4 fl oz/½ cup vegetable stock
salt and pepper • 2 tbsp chopped fresh coriander
(cilantro), to garnish

Paneer:

2.5 litres/4 pints/10 cups milk • 5 tbsp lemon juice
1 garlic clove, crushed (optional)
1 tbsp chopped fresh coriander (cilantro) (optional)

1 To make the paneer, bring the milk to a rolling boil in a large saucepan. Remove from the heat and stir in the lemon juice. Return to the heat for about 1 minute until the curds and whey separate. Remove from the heat. Line a colander with double thickness muslin and pour the mixture through the muslin. Add the garlic and coriander, if using. Squeeze all the liquid from the curds and leave to drain. Transfer to a dish, cover with a plate and weights and leave overnight in the refrigerator.

2 Cut the pressed paneer into small cubes. Heat the oil in a large frying pan (skillet), add the paneer cubes and fry until golden on all sides. Remove from the pan and drain on paper towels.

3 Pour off some of the oil, leaving 4 tablespoons in the pan. Add the onions, garlic and ginger and fry for 5 minutes, stirring frequently.

Stir in the garam masala, turmeric and chilli powder and fry for 2 minutes. Add the peas, tomatoes and stock, and season. Cover and simmer for 10 minutes, stirring, until the onion is tender.

4 Add the fried paneer cubes and cook for a further 5 minutes. Taste and adjust the seasoning, if necessary. Sprinkle with the coriander (cilantro) and serve at once.

Peshwari Naan

**A tandoor oven throws out a ferocious heat;
for an authentic effect, leave your grill
(broiler) on for a long time before starting.**

SERVES 4

50 ml / 2 fl oz / ¼ cup warm water
pinch of sugar • ½ tsp active dried yeast
500 g / 1 lb 2 oz / 4 cups strong white flour • ½ tsp salt
50 ml / 2 fl oz / ¼ cup natural yogurt
2 crisp, green apples, peeled, cooked and puréed
60 g / 2 oz / ⅓ cup sultanas (golden raisins)
60 g / 2 oz / ½ cup flaked (slivered) almonds
1 tbsp coriander (cilantro) leaves • 2 tbsp grated coconut

1 Combine the water and sugar in a bowl and sprinkle over the yeast. Leave for 5–10 minutes, until the yeast has dissolved and the mixture is foamy.

2 Put the flour and salt into a large bowl and make a well in the centre. Pour in the yeast mixture and yogurt to the bowl. Draw the flour into the liquid, until all the flour is absorbed. Mix together, adding enough tepid water to form a soft dough, about 150 ml / ¼ pint / ⅔ cup. Turn out on to a floured board and knead for 10 minutes until smooth and elastic. Put into an oiled bowl, cover with a cloth and leave for 3 hours in a warm place, or in the fridge overnight. Line the grill (broiler) pan with foil, shiny side up.

3 Divide the dough into 4 pieces and roll each piece out to a 20 cm/8 inch oval on a floured surface. Pull one end out into a teardrop shape, about 5 mm/ ¼ inch thick. Prick all over with a fork.

4 Brush both sides of the bread with oil. Place under a preheated grill (broiler) at the highest setting. Cook for 3 minutes, turn the bread over and cook for a

further 3 minutes until lightly browned all over.

5 Spread a teaspoonful of the apple purée all over the bread, then sprinkle over a quarter of the sultanas (golden raisins), the flaked (slivered) almonds, the coriander (cilantro) leaves and the coconut. Repeat with the remaining 3 ovals of dough.

Desserts

A cool, refreshing dessert is exactly what is required after serving a selection of the hot and spicy recipes in this book. The simplest and often most appreciated dessert after a hot curry is chilled fruit, or a cooling kulfi or ice-cream; the mango variety is featured in this chapter.

Mango Ice Cream

**This delicious ice cream makes the perfect
ending to a hot and spicy meal.**

SERVES 4

*150 ml/¼ pint/⅔ cup single (light) cream • 2 egg yolks
½ tsp cornflour (cornstarch) • 1 tsp water
2 × 400 g/14 oz cans of mango slices in syrup, drained
1 tbsp lime or lemon juice
150 ml/¼ pint/⅔ cup double (heavy) cream
sprigs of mint, to decorate*

1 Heat the cream in a saucepan until hot (not allowing it to boil). Place the egg yolks in a bowl with the cornflour (cornstarch) and water and mix until smooth. Pour the cream on to the egg yolk mixture, while stirring.

2 Return the mixture to the pan and place over a low heat, stirring constantly until the mixture thickens and coats the back of a wooden spoon (do not hurry this process or the mixture will overcook). Pour into a bowl.

3 Purée the drained mango slices in a blender or food processor until smooth, or chop finely, mash with a fork and push through a sieve. Mix with the custard and stir in the lime juice. Whip the double (heavy) cream until peaks form. Fold into the mango mixture.

4 Transfer the mixture to a loaf tin or shallow freezerproof container. Cover and freeze for 2–3 hours or until half-frozen. Turn the mixture into a bowl and mash well with a fork until smooth. Return to the container, cover and freeze again until firm.

5 Transfer the container of ice cream to the main compartment of the refrigerator for about 30 minutes before serving. Scoop or spoon the ice cream into serving dishes and decorate with sprigs of mint.

Saffron-Spiced Rice Pudding

This rich and comforting pudding is cooked in milk delicately flavoured with saffron and cinnamon.

SERVES 4–5

600 ml/1 pint/2½ cups milk
several pinches of saffron strands, finely crushed
60 g/2 oz/¼ cup short-grain (pudding) rice
1 cinnamon stick or piece of cassia bark
45 g/1½ oz/3 tbsp sugar
30 g/1 oz/¼ cup seedless raisins or sultanas (golden raisins)
30 g/1 oz/¼ cup ready-soaked dried apricots, chopped
1 egg, beaten
75 ml/3 fl oz/⅓ cup single (light) cream
15 g/½ oz/1 tbsp butter, diced
15 g/½ oz/2 tbsp flaked (slivered) almonds
freshly grated nutmeg, for sprinkling
cream (optional), to serve

1 Place the milk and crushed saffron in a non-stick saucepan and bring to the boil. Stir in the rice and cinnamon stick, reduce the heat and simmer very gently, uncovered, for 25 minutes, stirring frequently until the rice is tender.

2 Remove the pan from the heat and discard the cinnamon stick. Stir in the sugar, raisins and apricots, then beat in the egg, cream and diced butter.

3 Transfer the mixture to a greased ovenproof pie or flan dish, sprinkle with the almonds and freshly grated nutmeg, to taste. Place in a preheated oven, 160°C/325°F/Gas Mark 3, for 25–30 minutes until set and lightly golden. Serve hot with extra cream, if wished.

Sweet Carrot Halva

**This nutritious dessert, made from
grated carrots simmered in milk,
is flavoured with spices, nuts
and raisins.**

SERVES 4

*750 g/ 1½ lb carrots, grated
750 ml/ 1¼ pints/ 3 cups milk
1 cinnamon stick or piece of cassia bark (optional)
4 tbsp vegetable ghee or oil
60 g/ 2 oz/ ⅓ cup sugar
30 g/ 1 oz/ ¼ cup unsalted pistachio nuts, chopped
30–50 g/ 1–2 oz/ ¼–½ cup blanched almonds,
flaked (slivered) or chopped
60 g/ 2 oz/ ⅓ cup seedless raisins
seeds from 8 cardamom pods, crushed
double (heavy) cream or yogurt, to serve*

1 Put the grated carrots, milk and cinnamon or cassia, if using, into a large, heavy-based saucepan and bring to the boil. Reduce the heat to a simmer and cook, uncovered, for 35–40 minutes, or until thickened (with no milk remaining). Stir the mixture frequently during cooking to prevent it sticking. Remove the cinnamon stick.

2 Heat the ghee or oil in a non-stick frying pan (skillet), add the carrot mixture and stir-fry over a medium heat for about 5 minutes or until the carrots take on a glossy sheen.

3 Add the sugar, pistachios, almonds, raisins and crushed cardamom seeds, mix well and continue frying for a further 3–4 minutes, stirring frequently. Serve warm or cold with cream or yogurt.

Thai-Style Bananas

The Thais rarely finish a meal with an elaborate dessert, preferring a selection of tropical fruits. This is one of the mouth-watering exceptions.

SERVES 6

3 tbsp shredded fresh coconut
60 g/ 2 oz/ 4 tbsp unsalted butter
1 tbsp grated ginger root
grated zest of 1 orange
6 bananas
6 tbsp orange liqueur (Cointreau or Grand Marnier, for example)
3 tsp toasted sesame seeds
lime slices, to decorate
ice-cream, to serve (optional)

1 Heat a small non-stick frying pan (skillet) until hot. Add the coconut and cook, stirring, for about 1 minute until lightly coloured. Remove from the pan and allow to cool.

2 Heat the butter in a large frying pan (skillet) until it melts. Add the ginger and orange zest and mix well.

3 Peel and slice the bananas lengthways (and halve if they are very large). Place the bananas cut-side down in the butter mixture and cook for 1–2 minutes or until the sauce mixture starts to become sticky. Turn to coat in the sauce. Remove the bananas from the pan and place on warmed serving plates. Keep warm.

4 Return the pan to the heat and add the orange liqueur, stirring well to blend. Ignite with a taper, allow the flames to die down, then pour the liquid over the bananas.

5 Sprinkle with the coconut and sesame seeds and serve at once, decorated with slices of lime.

Baked Coconut Rice Pudding

A wonderful baked rice pudding cooked with flavoursome coconut milk and a little lime rind. Serve hot or chilled with fresh or stewed fruit.

SERVES 4

90 g / 3 oz / scant ⅓ cup short or round-grain pudding rice
600 ml / 1 pint / 2½ cups coconut milk
300 ml / ½ pint / 1¼ cups milk
1 large strip lime rind
60 g / 2 oz / ⅓ cup caster sugar
knob of butter
pinch of ground star anise (optional)
fresh or stewed fruit, to serve

1 Heat the oven to 160°C/325°F/Gas Mark 2. Mix the rice with the coconut milk, milk, lime rind and sugar.

2 Pour the rice mixture into a lightly-greased 1.5 litre/ 2½ pint shallow ovenproof dish and dot the surface with a little butter. Bake in a preheated oven at 160°C/ 325°F/Gas Mark 3 for about 30 minutes.

3 Remove and discard the strip of lime. Stir the pudding well, add a pinch of ground star anise, if using, return to the oven and cook for 1–2 hours or until almost all the milk has been absorbed and a golden brown skin has formed on the top of the pudding. (Cover the top of the pudding with foil if it starts to brown too much towards the end of the cooking time.)

4 Serve the pudding warm or chilled with fresh or stewed fruit.

Pancakes Polamai

These Thai pancakes are filled with an exotic array of tropical fruits.

SERVES 4

*125 g/ 4 oz/ 1 cup plain flour • pinch of salt • 1 egg
1 egg yolk • 300 ml/ ½ pint/ 1¼ cups coconut milk
4 tsp vegetable oil, plus oil for frying
flowers or sprigs of mint, to decorate*

Filling:

*1 banana • 1 paw-paw (papaya) • juice of 1 lime
2 passion fruit • 1 mango, peeled, stoned and sliced
4 lychees, stoned and halved • 1–2 tbsp honey*

1 To make the batter, sift the flour into a bowl with the salt. Make a well in the centre, add the egg and yolk and a little coconut milk. Gradually draw the flour into the egg mixture, beating well and gradually adding the remaining coconut milk to make a smooth batter. Add the oil and mix well. Cover and chill for 30 minutes.

2 To make the filling, peel and slice the banana and put in a bowl. Peel and slice the paw-paw (papaya), remove the seeds then cut into bite-sized chunks. Add to the banana with the lime juice and mix to coat.

3 Cut the passion fruit in half, scoop out the flesh and seeds and add to the banana mixture. Add the mango, lychees and honey and mix.

4 To make the pancakes, heat a little oil in a 15 cm/6 inch crêpe or frying pan (skillet). Pour in enough of the pancake batter to cover the base of the pan and tilt it so that it spreads thinly and evenly. Cook until the pancake is just set and the underside is lightly browned, turn and briefly cook the other side. Remove from the pan and keep warm. Repeat to make a total of 8 pancakes.

5 To serve, place a little of the prepared fruit filling along the centre of each pancake and, using both hands, roll it into a cone shape. Lay the pancakes seam-side down on warmed serving plates, allowing 2 pancakes per serving. Serve at once, decorated with flowers and mint sprigs, if liked.

Mangoes with Sticky Rice

This traditional South-east Asian dessert has to be included in this book, as every Thai cook knows how to make it, and it will round off any Thai meal perfectly.

SERVES 4

125 g/ 4 oz/ 1 cup glutinous (sticky) rice or short-grain pudding rice
250 ml/ 8 fl oz/ 1 cup coconut milk
60 g/ 2 oz /⅓ cup light muscovado sugar
½ tsp salt • 1 tsp sesame seeds, toasted
4 ripe mangoes, peeled, halved, stoned (pitted) and sliced

1 Put the rice into a colander and rinse well with plenty of cold water until the water runs clear. Transfer the rice to a large bowl, cover with cold water and leave to soak overnight, or for at least 12 hours. Drain well.

2 Line a bamboo basket or steamer with muslin (cheesecloth) or finely woven cotton cloth. Add the rice and steam over a pan of gently simmering water until the rice is tender, about 40 minutes. Remove from the heat and transfer the rice to a bowl.

3 Reserve 4 tablespoons of the coconut milk and put the remainder into a small saucepan with the sugar and salt. Heat and simmer gently for about 8 minutes until reduced by about one third.

4 Pour the coconut milk mixture over the rice, fluffing up the rice so that the mixture is absorbed. Set aside for 10–15 minutes.

5 Pack the rice into individual moulds and then invert them on to serving plates. Spoon a little reserved coconut milk over each mound and sprinkle with the sesame seeds. Arrange the sliced mango on the plates and serve, decorated with pieces of mango cut into shapes with tiny cutters.

Index

Aubergines (eggplants):
  aubergine (eggplant) dipping
    platter 148
  aubergine (eggplant) in saffron
    sauce 174
  brindil bhaji 216
Aviyal 160

Bajan fish 112-13
Bamboo shoots with cucumber 154
Bananas, Thai-style 230
Bang-bang chicken 60
Bean-sprouts: spring rolls 28
Beans:
  beef with beans 80
  mixed bean stir-fry 164
Beef:
  beef & bok choy 90
  beef & chilli black bean
    sauce 82-3
  beef with beans 80
  green beef curry 92
  Ma-Po tofu (bean curd) 86
  oyster sauce beef 84
  peppered beef cashew 88
  red spiced beef 76
  sukiyaki beef 78
Biryani, lamb 96-7
Black bean sauce, beef & chilli 82-3
Bok choy, beef & 90
Bread:
  Peshwari naan 220-1
Brindil bhaji 216
Broccoli:
  gingered broccoli with orange 166
Butterfly prawns (shrimp) 46

Cabbage, caraway 158
Cannellini beans:
  beef with beans 80
Carrot halva 228
Channa dal 214
Chatuchak fried rice 202
Cheese:
  muttar paneer 218-19
Chicken:
  bang-bang chicken 60

chicken jalfrezi 50
chicken soup with almonds 12
chicken tikka masala 54-5
chicken with peanut sauce 56-7
fat horses 36
green chilli chicken 66
kung po chicken with cashew
  nuts 58
lemon chicken 62
peanut sesame chicken 68
red chicken curry 64
tandoori chicken 52
three-flavour soup 24-5
Chillies:
  green chilli chicken 66
Chinese fried rice 196-7
Chinese hot salad 156
Chinese leaves, braised 168
Chow mein, seafood 208-9
Coconut milk:
  baked coconut rice
    pudding 232
Coconut rice 192
Courgettes (zucchini), deep-fried 40
Crab:
  baked crab with ginger 142
  curried crab 130
  fat horses 36
  rice with crab & mussels 190
Curries:
  chicken tikka masala 54-5
  curried crab 130
  curried okra 172
  green beef curry 92
  green chilli chicken 66
  green fish curry 124
  king prawns (jumbo shrimp) in red
    curry sauce 132
  Massaman curried rice 204-5
  red chicken curry 64
  red curry fish cakes 120
  vindaloo curry 100-1

Desserts 223-36
Duck:
  aromatic & crispy duck 74-5
  duck with ginger & lime 70

duck with lime & kiwi
fruit 72-3

Eggplants see Aubergines
Eggs:
  egg fried rice 182
  egg fu-yung with rice 184-5

Fat horses 36
Fish & seafood 109-44
  braised fish fillets 122-3
  fish & vegetable soup 14
  fish with saffron sauce 114-15
  green fish curry 124
  red curry fish cakes 120
Five-spice lamb 94
Fruit:
  pancakes polamai 234-5

Green beef curry 92
Green chilli chicken 66
Green fish curry 124
Green rice 200

Halva, sweet carrot 228
Ham:
  three-flavour soup 24-5
Hot & sour soup 22

Ice cream, mango 224
Indian prawns (shrimp) 42

Kaffir lime mussels with lemon
  grass 134
Kashmiri spinach 178
Kiwi fruit, duck with lime & 72-3
Kung po chicken with cashew
  nuts 58

Lamb:
  five-spice lamb 94
  lamb biryani 96-7
  lamb do pyaza 98
Lemon chicken 62
Little golden parcels 34
Lotus leaves, fragrant steamed rice
  in 186-7

Ma-Po tofu (bean curd) 86
Mangoes:
  ice cream 224
  with sticky rice 236

Masala fried fish 126
Massaman curried rice 204-5
Meat & poultry 49-106
Money bags 30
Monkfish:
  Bajan fish 112-13
Mushroom pakoras, garlicky 170
Mussels:
  kaffir lime mussels with lemon
    grass 134
  mussel morsels 40-1
Muttar paneer 218-19

Naan, Peshwari 220-1
Nasi goreng 188
Noodles:
  seafood chow mein 208-9
  Singapore-style rice
    noodles 210
Nuts, spiced 40

Okra, curried 172
Onions:
  lamb do pyaza 98
Oyster sauce beef 84

Pakoras, garlicky mushroom 170
Pancakes polamai 234-5
Paneer, muttar 218-19
Paw-paw (papaya) salad 152
Peanuts:
  chicken with peanut sauce 56-7
  peanut sesame chicken 68
Peppered beef cashew 88
Peshwari naan 220-1
Pilau, spiced basmati 206
Plaice:
  masala fried fish 126
Pork:
  deep-fried spare ribs 102
  nasi goreng 188
  pork & prawn (shrimp) sesame
    toasts 32-3
  pork & Szechuan vegetable
    soup 26
  pork balls with minted
    sauce 104-5
  stir-fried pork with
    vegetables 106
  vindaloo curry 100-1
Potatoes, fried spiced 176
Poultry & meat 49-106

Prawns (shrimp):
  butterfly prawns (shrimp) 46
  fried rice with prawns
   (shrimp) 194
  Indian prawns (shrimp) 42
  king prawns (jumbo shrimp) in red
   curry sauce 132
  pork & prawn (shrimp) sesame
   toasts 32-3
  prawn (shrimp) bhuna 128
  prawn (shrimp) soup 16
  prawns (shrimp) in sauce 44-5
  shrimp rolls 136
  Szechuan prawns (shrimp) 138
  three-flavour soup 24-5

Red chicken curry 64
Red curry fish cakes 120
Red spiced beef 76
Rice:
  baked coconut rice pudding 232
  Chatuchak fried rice 202
  Chinese fried rice 196-7
  coconut rice 192
  egg fried rice 182
  egg fu-yung with rice 184-5
  fragrant steamed rice in lotus
   leaves 186-7
  fried rice with prawns
   (shrimp) 194
  green rice 200
  lamb biryani 96-7
  mangoes with sticky rice 236
  Massaman curried rice 204-5
  nasi goreng 188
  rice with crab & mussels 190
  saffron-spiced rice pudding 226
  spiced basmati pilau 206
  Thai jasmine rice 198

Saffron-spiced rice pudding 226
Salads:
  Chinese hot salad 156
  paw-paw (papaya) salad 152
Salmon:
  sesame salmon & cream sauce 116
Samosas 38-9
Scallops, spiced 144
Seafood & fish 109-44
Seafood chow mein 208-9
Shrimp see Prawns
Singapore-style rice noodles 210

Sole paupiette 110-11
Soups 12-26
Spicy bites 40-1
Spinach:
  Kashmiri spinach 178
  spinach & tofu soup 18
Spring rolls 28
  shrimp rolls 136
Squid flowers, fried 140
Sukiyaki beef 78
Sweet & sour vegetables 162-3
Sweetcorn patties 150
Szechuan prawns (shrimp) 138

Tandoori chicken 52
Thai jasmine rice 198
Thai-style bananas 230
Three-flavour soup 24-5
Tofu (bean curd):
  Ma-Po tofu (bean curd) 86
  spinach & tofu (bean curd)
   soup 18
Trout:
  fish with ginger butter 118
Tuna:
  samosas 38-9

Vegetables 147-78
  aviyal 160
  pork & Szechuan vegetable
   soup 26
  stir-fried pork with vegetables 106
  sweet & sour vegetables 162-3
Vindaloo curry 100-1

Water chestnuts:
  little golden parcels 34
Wonton soup 20

Yellow split peas:
  casserole 212-13
  channa dal 214

Zucchini see Courgettes

Index compiled by Hilary Bird